HOME UNIVERSITY LIBRARY
OF MODERN KNOWLEDGE

No. 103

Editors:

HERBERT FISHER, M.A., F.B.A.
Prof. GILBERT MURRAY, Litt.D.
LL.D., F.B.A.
Prof. J. ARTHUR THOMSON, M.A.
Prof. WILLIAM T. BREWSTER, M.A.

POLITICAL THOUGHT
IN ENGLAND

FROM
LOCKE TO BENTHAM

BY

HAROLD J. LASKI
SOMETIME EXHIBITIONER OF NEW COLLEGE, OXFORD, OF THE
DEPARTMENT OF HISTORY IN HARVARD UNIVERSITY,
AUTHOR OF STUDIES IN THE PROBLEM OF
SOVEREIGNTY AND AUTHORITY IN
THE MODERN STATE

GREENWOOD PRESS, PUBLISHERS
WESTPORT, CONNECTICUT

The Library of Congress has catalogued this publication as follows:

Library of Congress Cataloging in Publication Data

Laski, Harold Joseph, 1893-1950.
   Political thought in England from Locke to Bentham.

   Reprint of the 1920 ed., which was issued as no. 103
of the Home university library of modern knowledge.
   Bibliography: p.
   1. Political science—History—Great Britain.
I. Title.
JA84.G7L3   1973   320.9'42   72-9086
ISBN 0-8371-6570-9

Originally published in 1920 by Henry Holt and Company,
New York

Reprinted by Greenwood Press, Inc.

First Greenwood reprinting 1973
Second Greenwood reprinting 1977

Library of Congress catalog card number 72-9086
ISBN 0-8371-6570-9

Printed in the United States of America

NOTE

IT is impossible for me to publish this book without some expression of the debt it owes to Leslie Stephen's *History of the English Thought in the Eighteenth Century.* It is almost insolent to praise such work; but I may be permitted to say that no one can fully appreciate either its wisdom or its knowledge who has not had to dig among the original texts.

Were so small a volume worthy to bear a dedication, I should associate it with the name of my friend Walter Lippmann. He and I have so often discussed the substance of its problems that I am certain a good deal of what I feel to be my own is, where it has merit, really his. This volume is thus in great part a tribute to him; though there is little that can repay such friendship as he gives.

H. J. L.

HARVARD UNIVERSITY
Sept. 15, 1919

CONTENTS

CHAPTER   PAGE

I. INTRODUCTION 7

II. THE PRINCIPLES OF THE REVOLUTION   24

III. CHURCH AND STATE 77

IV. THE ERA OF STAGNATION . . . 127

V. SIGNS OF CHANGE 159

VI. BURKE 213

VII. THE FOUNDATIONS OF ECONOMIC
LIBERALISM 281

BIBLIOGRAPHY 317

INDEX 321

CHAPTER I

INTRODUCTION

THE eighteenth century may be said to
begin with the Revolution of 1688; for,
with its completion, the dogma of Divine
Right disappeared for ever from English
politics. Its place was but partially filled
until Hume and Burke supplied the outlines of a new philosophy. For the observer of this age can hardly fail, as he
notes its relative barrenness of abstract
ideas, to be impressed by the large part
Divine Right must have played in the politics of the succeeding century. Its very
absoluteness made for keen partisanship
on the one side and the other. It could
produce at once the longwinded rhap-
sodies of Filmer and, by repulsion, the
wearisome reiterations of Algernon Sidney. Once the foundations of Divine
Right had been destroyed by Locke, the
basis of passionate controversy was ab-

sent. The theory of a social contract never produced in England the enthusiasm it evoked in France, for the simple reason that the main objective of Rousseau and his disciples had already been secured there by other weapons. And this has perhaps given to the eighteenth century an urbaneness from which its predecessor was largely free. Sermons are perhaps the best test of such a change; and it is a relief to move from the addresses bristling with Suarez and Bellarmine to the noble exhortations of Bishop Butler. Not until the French Revolution were ultimate dogmas again called into question; and it is about them only that political speculation provokes deep feeling. The urbanity, indeed, is not entirely new. The Restoration had heralded its coming, and the tone of Halifax has more in common with Bolingbroke and Hume than with Hobbes and Filmer. Nor has the eighteenth century an historical profundity to compare with that of the zealous pamphleteers in the seventeenth. Heroic archivists like Prynne find very different substitutes in brilliant journalists like Defoe, and if Dalrymple and Blackstone are respectable, they bear no comparison with masters like Selden and Sir Henry Spelman. Yet urbanity must not deceive us. The eighteenth century has an importance in English politics which the comparative absence of systematic speculation can not conceal. If its large constitutional outlines had been traced by a preceding age, its administrative detail had still to be secured. The process was very gradual; and the attempt of George III to arrest it produced the splendid effort of Edmund Burke. Locke's work may have been not seldom confused and stumbling; but it gave to the principle of consent a permanent place in English politics. It is the age which saw the crystallization of the party-system, and therein it may perhaps lay claim to have recognized what Bagehot called the vital principle of representative government. Few discussions of the sphere of government have been so productive as that in which Adam Smith gave a new basis to economic science. Few controversies have, despite its dullness, so carefully investigated the eternal problem of Church and State as that to which Hoadly's bishopric contributed its name.

De Lolme is the real parent of that inter-
pretative analysis which has, in Bagehot's
hands, become not the least fruitful type
of political method. Blackstone, in a real
sense, may be called the ancestor of Professor Dicey. The very calmness of the
atmosphere only the more surely paved
the way for the surprising novelties of
Godwin and the revolutionists.

Nor must we neglect the relation between its ethics and its politics. The
eighteenth century school of British mor-
alists has suffered somewhat beside the
greater glories of Berkeley and Hume.
Yet it was a great work to which they
bent their effort, and they knew its greatness. The deistic controversy involved a
fresh investigation of the basis of morals;
and it is to the credit of the investigators
that they attempted to provide it in social
terms. It is, indeed, one of the primary
characteristics of the British mind to be interested in problems of conduct rather
than of thought. The seventeenth century had, for the most part, been interested in theology and government; and its
preoccupation, in both domains, with
supernatural sanctions, made its conclu-

sions unfitted for a period dominated by
rationalism. Locke regarded his *Human
Understanding* as the preliminary to an
ethical enquiry; and Hume seems to have
considered his *Principles of Morals* the
most vital of his works. It may be true,
as the mordant insight of Mark Pattison
suggested, that "those periods in which
morals have been represented as the
proper study of man, and his only business, have been periods of spiritual abasement and poverty." Certainly no one will
be inclined to claim for the eighteenth century the spiritual idealism of the seventeenth, though Law and Bishop Wilson
and the Wesleyan revival will make us
generalize with caution. But the truth
was that theological ethics had become
empty and inadequate, and the problem
was therefore urgent. That is why
Shaftesbury, Hutcheson, Hume and
Adam Smith — to take only men of the
first eminence — were thinking not less
for politics than for ethics when they
sought to justify the ways of man to man.
For all of them saw that a theory of society is impossible without the provision
of psychological foundations; and those

must, above all, result in a theory of conduct if the social bond is to be maintained.
That sure insight is, of course, one current
only in a greater English stream which
reaches back to Hobbes at its source and
forward to T. H. Green at perhaps its
fullest. Its value is its denial of politics
as a science distinct from other human
relations; and that is why Adam Smith
can write of moral sentiments no less than
of the wealth of nations. The eighteenth
century saw clearly that each aspect of
social life must find its place in the political equation.

Yet it is undoubtedly an age of methods
rather than of principles; and, as such its
peaceful prosperity was well suited to its
questions. Problems of technique, such
as the cabinet and the Bank of England
required the absence of passionate debate
if they were in any fruitful fashion to be
solved. Nor must the achievement of the
age in politics be minimized. It was, of
course, a complacent time; but we ought
to note that foreigners of distinction did
not wonder at its complacency. Voltaire
and Montesquieu look back to England in
the eighteenth century for the substance

of political truths. The American colonies
took alike their methods and their arguments from English ancestors; and Burke
provided them with the main elements of
justification. The very quietness, indeed,
of the time was the natural outcome of a
century of storm; and England surely had
some right to be contented when her political system was compared with the governments of France and Germany. Not,
indeed, that the full fruit of the Revolution was gathered. The principle of consent came, in practice and till 1760, to
mean the government of the Whig Oligarchy; and the *Extraordinary Black
Book* remains to tell us what happened
when George III gave the Tory party a
new lease of power. There is throughout
the time an over-emphasis upon the value
of order, and a not unnatural tendency to
confound the private good of the governing class with the general welfare of the
state. It became the fixed policy of Walpole to make prosperity the mask for political stagnation. He turned political debate from principles to personalities, and
a sterile generation was the outcome of
his cunning.

Not that this barrenness is without its
compensations. The theories of the Revolution had exhausted their fruitfulness
within a generation. The constitutional
ideas of the seventeenth century had no
substance for an England where Angli-
canism and agriculture were beginning to
lose the rigid outlines of overwhelming
predominance. What was needed was the
assurance of safety for the Church that
her virtue might be tested in the light of
nonconformist practice on the one hand,
and the new rationalism on the other.
What was needed also was the expansion
of English commerce into the new
channels opened for it by the victories of
Chatham. Mr. Chief Justice Holt had
given it the legal categories it would require; and Hume and Adam Smith were
to explain that commerce might grow with
small danger to agricultural prosperity.
Beneath the apparent calm of Walpole's
rule new forces were fast stirring. That
can be seen on every side. The sturdy
morality of Johnson, the new literary
forms of Richardson and Fielding, the
theatre which Garrick founded upon the
ruins produced by Collier's indignation,

the revival of which Law and Wesley are the great symbols, show that the stagnation was sleep rather than death. The needed events of shock were close at hand. The people of England would never have discovered the real meaning of 1688 if George III had not denied its principles. When he enforced the resignation of the elder Pitt the theories at once of Edmund Burke and English radicalism were born; for the *Present Discontents* and the *Society for the Support of the Bill of Rights* are the dawn of a splendid recovery. And they made possible the speculative ferment which showed that England was at last awake to the meaning of Montesquieu and Rousseau. Just as the shock of the Lancastrian wars produced the Tudor despotism, so did the turmoil of civil strife produce the complacency of the eighteenth century. But the peace of the Tudors was the death-bed of the Stuarts; and it was the stagnant optimism of the early eighteenth century which made possible the birth of democratic England.

The atmosphere of the time, in fact, is deep-rooted in the conditions of the past. Locke could not have written had not

Hobbes and Filmer defended in set terms the ideal of despotic government. He announced the advent of the modern system of parliamentary government; and from his time the debate has been rather of the conditions under which it is to work, than of the foundations upon which it is based. Burke, for example, wrote what constitutes the supreme analysis of the statesman's art. Adam Smith discussed in what fashion the prosperity of peoples could be best advanced. From Locke, that is to say, the subject of discussion is rather *politik* than *staatslehre*. The great debate inaugurated by the Reformation ceased when Locke had outlined an intelligible basis for parliamentary government. Hume, Bolingbroke, Burke, are all of them concerned with the detail of political arrangement in a fashion which presupposes the acceptance of a basis previously known. Burke, indeed, toward the latter part of his life, awoke to the realization that men were dissatisfied with the traditional substance of the State. But he met the new desires with hate instead of understanding, and the Napoleonic wars drove the current of democratic opinion underground. Hall and Owen and Hodgskin inherited the thoughts of Ogilvie and Spence and Paine; and if they did not give them substance, at least they gave them form for a later time.

Nor is the reason for this preoccupation far to seek. The advance of English politics in the preceding two centuries was mainly an advance of structure; yet relative at least to continental fact, it appeared liberal enough to hide the disharmonies of its inner content. The King was still a mighty influence. The power of the aristocracy was hardly broken until the Reform Bill of 1867. The Church continued to dominate the political aspect of English religious life until, after 1832, new elements alien from her ideals were introduced into the House of Commons. The conditions of change lay implicit in the Industrial Revolution, when a new class of men attained control of the nation's economic power. Only then was a realignment of political forces essential. Only then, that is to say, had the time arrived for a new theory of the State.

The political ideas of the eigtheenth

century are thus in some sort a comment upon the system established by the Revolution; and that is, in its turn, the product of the struggle between Parliament and Crown in the preceding age. But we cannot understand the eighteenth century, or its theories, unless we realize that its temper was still dominantly aristocratic. From no accusation were its statesmen more anxious to be free than from that of a belief in democratic government. Whether Whigs or Tories were in power, it was always the great families who ruled. For them the Church, at least in its higher branches, existed; and the difference between nobleman and commoner at Oxford is as striking as it is hideous to this generation. For them also literature and the theatre made their display; and if Dr. Johnson could heap an immortal contumely upon the name of patron, we all know of the reverence he felt in the presence of the king. Divine Right and non-resistance were dead, but they had not died without a struggle. Freedom of the press and legal equality may have been obtained; but it was not until the passage of Fox's Libel Act that the first became se-

cure, and Mr. and Mrs. Hammond have
recently illumined for us the inward meaning of the second. The populace might,
on occasion, be strong enough to force the
elder Pitt upon an unwilling king, or to
shout for Wilkes and liberty against the
unconstitutional usurpation of the mon-
arch-ridden House of Commons. Such
outbursts are yet the exception to the pre-
vailing temper. The deliberations of
Parliament were still, at least technically,
a secret; and membership therein, save for
one or two anomalies like Westminster
and Bristol, was still the private possession of a privileged class. The Revolution, in fact, meant less an abstract and
general freedom, than a special release
from the arbitrary will of a stupid monarch who aroused against himself every
deep-seated prejudice of his generation.
The England which sent James II upon
his travels may be, as Hume pointed out,
reduced to a pathetic fragment even of its
electorate. The masses were unknown
and undiscovered, or, where they emerged,
it was either to protest against some
wise reform like Walpole's Excise
Scheme, or to become, as in Goldsmith

and Cowper and Crabbe, the object of half-pitying poetic sentiment. How deep-rooted was the notion of aristocratic control was to be shown when France turned into substantial fact Rousseau's demand for freedom. The protest of Burke against its supposed anarchy swept England like a flame; and only a courageous handful could be found to protest against Pitt's prostitution of her freedom.

Such an age could make but little pretence to discovery; and, indeed, it is most largely absent from its speculation. In its political ideas this is necessarily and especially the case. For the State is at no time an unchanging organization; it reflects with singular exactness the dominating ideas of its environment. That division into government and subjects which is its main characteristic is here noteworthy for the narrowness of the class from which the government is derived, and the consistent inertia of those over whom it rules. There is curiously little controversy over the seat of sovereign power. That is with most men acknowledged to reside in the king in Parliament. What balance of forces is necessary to its most

perfect equilibrium may arouse dissension
when George III forgets the result of half
a century's evolution. Junius may have
to explain in invective what Burke magis-
trally demonstrated in terms of political
philosophy. But the deeper problems of
the state lay hidden until Bentham and
the revolutionists came to insist upon their
presence. That did not mean that the
eighteenth century was a soulless failure.
Rather did it mean that a period of transition had been successfully bridged. The
stage was set for a new effort simply because the theories of the older philosophy
no longer represented the facts at issue.

It was thus Locke only in this period
who confronted the general problems of
the modern State. Other thinkers assumed
his structure and dealt with the details he
left undetermined. The main problems,
the Church apart, arose when a foreigner
occupied the English throne and left the
methods of government to those who were
acquainted with them. That most happy
of all the happy accidents in English history made Walpole the fundamental
statesman of the time. He used his opportunity to the full. Inheriting the pos-

sibilities of the cabinet system he gave it
its modern expression by creating the
office of Prime Minister. The party-
system was already inevitable; and with
his advent to full power in 1727 we have
the characteristic outlines of English representative government. Thenceforward,
there are, on the whole, but three large
questions with which the age concerned
itself. Toleration had already been won
by the persistent necessities of two generations, and the noble determination of
William III; but the place of the Church
in the Revolution State and the nature of
that State were still undetermined.
Hoadly had one solution, Law another;
and the genial rationalism of the time,
coupled with the political affiliations of
the High Church party, combined to give
Hoadly the victory; but his opponents,
and Law especially, remained to be the
parents of a movement for ecclesiastical
freedom of which it has been the good fortune of Oxford to supply in each succeeding century the leaders. America pre-
sented again the problem of consent in the
special perspective of the imperial relation; and the decision which grew out of

the blundering obscurantism of the King enabled Burke nobly to restate and amply to revivify the principles of 1688. Chatham meanwhile had stumbled upon a vaster empire; and the industrial system which his effort quickened could not live under an economic régime which still bore traces of the narrow nationalism of the Tudors. No man was so emphatically representative of his epoch as Adam Smith; and no thinker has ever stated in such generous terms the answer of his time to the most vital of its questions. The answer, indeed, like all good answers, revealed rather the difficulty of the problem than' the prospect of its solution; though nothing so clearly heralded the new age that was coming than his repudiation of the past in terms of a real appreciation of it. The American War and the two great revolutions brought a new race of thinkers into being. The French seed at last produced its harvest. Bentham absorbed the purpose of Rousseau even while he rejected his methods. For a time, indeed, the heat and dust of war obscured the issue that Bentham raised. But the certainties of the future lay on his side.

CHAPTER II

THE PRINCIPLES OF THE REVOLUTION

I

THE English Revolution was in the main a protest against the attempt of James II to establish a despotism in alliance with France and Rome. It was almost entirely a movement of the aristocracy, and, for the most part, it was aristocratic opposition that it encountered. What it did was to make for ever impossible the thought of reunion with Rome and the theory that the throne could be established on any other basis than the consent of Parliament. For no one could pretend that William of Orange ruled by Divine Right. The scrupulous shrank from proclaiming the deposition of James; and the fiction that he had abdicated was not calculated to deceive even the warmest of William's adherents. An unconstitutional Parliament thereupon declared the throne

vacant; and after much negotiation
William and Mary were invited to occupy
it. To William the invitation was irresistible. It gave him the assistance of the
first maritime power in Europe against
the imperialism of Louis XIV. It en-
sured the survival of Protestantism
against the encroachments of an enemy
who never slumbered. Nor did England
find the new régime unwelcome. Every
widespread conviction of her people had
been wantonly outraged by the blundering
stupidity of James. If a large fraction of
the English Church held aloof from the
new order on technical grounds, the commercial classes gave it their warm support; and many who doubted in theory
submitted in practice. All at least were
conscious that a new era had dawned.

For William had come over with a definite purpose in view. James had wrought
havoc with what the Civil Wars had made
the essence of the English constitution;
and it had become important to define in
set terms the conditions upon which the
life of kings must in the future be regu-
lated. The reign of William is nothing
so much as the period of that definition;

and the fortunate discovery was made of the mechanisms whereby its translation into practice might be secured. The Bill of Rights (1689) and the Act of Settlement (1701) are the foundation-stones of the modern constitutional system.

What, broadly, was established was the dependence of the crown upon Parliament. Finance and the army were brought under Parliamentary control by the simple expedient of making its annual summons essential. The right of petition was re-affirmed; and the independence of the judges and ministerial responsibility were secured by the same act which forever excluded the legitimate heirs from their royal inheritance. It is difficult not to be amazed at the almost casual fashion in which so striking a revolution was effected. Not, indeed, that the solution worked easily at the outset. William remained to the end a foreigner, who could not understand the inwardness of English politics. It was the necessities of foreign policy which drove him to admit the immense possibilities of the party-system as also to accept his own best safeguard in the foundation of the Bank of England.

The Cabinet, towards the close of his reign, had already become the fundamental administrative instrument. Originally a committee of the Privy Council, it had no party basis until the ingenious Sunderland atoned for a score of dishonesties by insisting that the root of its efficiency would be found in its selection from a single party. William acquiesced but doubtfully; for, until the end of his life, he never understood why his ministers should not be a group of able counsellors chosen without reference to their political affiliations. Sunderland knew better for the simple reason that he belonged to that period when the Whigs and Tories had gambled against each other for their heads. He knew that no council-board could with comfort contain both himself and Halifax; just as William himself was to learn quite early that neither honor nor confidence could win unswerving support from John Churchill. There is a certain feverishness in the atmosphere of the reign which shows how many kept an anxious eye on St. Germain even while they attended the morning levee at Whitehall.

What secured the permanence of the

settlement was less the policy of William than the blunder of the French monarch. Patience, foresight and generosity had not availed to win for William more than a grudging recognition of his kingship. He had received only a half-hearted support for his foreign policy. The army, despite his protests, had been reduced; and the enforced return of his own Dutch Guards to Holland was deliberately conceived to cause him pain. But at the very moment when his strength seemed weakest James II died; and Louis XIV, despite written obligation, sought to comfort the last moments of his tragic exile by the falsely chivalrous recognition of the Old Pretender as the rightful English king. It was a terrible mistake. It did for William what no action of his own could ever have achieved. It suggested that England must receive its ruler at the hands of a foreign sovereign. The national pride of the people rallied to the cause for which William stood. He was king — so, at least in contrast to Louis' decision, it appeared — by their deliberate choice and the settlement of which he was the symbol would be maintained. Parliament granted

to William all that his foreign policy could
have demanded. His own death was only
the prelude to the victories of Marl-
borough. Those victories seemed to seal
the solution of 1688. A moment came
when sentiment and intrigue combined to
throw in jeopardy the Act of Settlement.
But Death held the stakes against the
gambler's throw of Bolingbroke; and the
accession of George I assured the permanence of Revolution principles.

II

The theorist of the Revolution is Locke;
and it was his conscious effort to justify
the innovations of 1688. He sought, as
he said, "to establish the throne of our
great Restorer, our present King William, and make good his title in the consent of the people." In the debate which
followed his argument remained unanswered, for the sufficient reason that it had
the common sense of the generation on his
side. Yet Locke has suffered not a little
at the hands of succeeding thinkers.
Though his influence upon his own time
was immense; though Montesquieu owed

to him the acutest of his insights; though
the principles of the American Revolution are in large part an acknowledged
adoption of his own; he has become one of
the political classics who are taken for
granted rather than read. It is a profound and regrettable error. Locke may
not possess the clarity and ruthless logic
of Hobbes, or the genius for compressing
into a phrase the experience of a lifetime
which makes Burke the first of English
political thinkers. He yet stated more
clearly than either the general problem of
the modern State. Hobbes, after all,
worked with an impossible psychology
and sought no more than the prescription
against disorder. Burke wrote rather a
text-book for the cautious administrator
than a guide for the liberal statesman.
But Locke saw that the main problem of
the State is the conquest of freedom and it
was for its definition in terms of individual
good that he above all strove.

Much, doubtless, of his neglect is due
to the medium in which he worked. He
wrote at a time when the social contract
seemed the only possible retort to the
theory of Divine Right. He so empha-

sized the principle of consent that when contractualism came in its turn to be discarded, it was discovered that Locke suffered far more than Hobbes by the change so made. For Hobbes cared nothing for the contract so long as strong government could be shown to be implicit in the natural badness of men, while Locke assumed their goodness and made his contract essential to their opportunity for moral expression. Nor did he, like Rousseau, seize upon the organic nature of the State. To him the State was always a mere aggregate, and the convenient simplicity of majority-rule solved, for him, the vital political problems. But Rousseau was translated into the complex dialectic of Hegel and lived to become the parent of theories he would have doubtless been the first to disown. Nor was Locke aided by his philosophic outlook. Few great thinkers have so little perceived the psychological foundations of politics. What he did was rather to fasten upon the great institutional necessity of his time — the provision of channels of assent — and emphasize its importance to the exclusion of all other factors. The problem is in fact

more complex; and the solution he indi-
cated became so natural a part of the political fabric that the value of his emphasis
upon its import was largely forgotten
when men again took up the study of
foundations.

John Locke was born at Wrington in
Somerset on the 29th of August, 1632.
His father was clerk to the county jus-
tices and acted as a captain in a cavalry
regiment during the Civil War. Though
he suffered heavy losses, he was able to
give his son as good an education as the
time afforded. Westminster under Dr.
Busby may not have been the gentlest of
academies, but at least it provided Locke
with an admirable training in the classics.
He himself, indeed, in the *Thoughts on
Education* doubted the value of such ex-
ercises; nor does he seem to have conceived
any affection for Oxford whither he proceeded in 1652 as a junior student of
Christ Church. The university was then
under the Puritan control of Dr. John
Owen; but not even his effort to redeem
the university from its reputation for intellectual laxity rescued it from the
"wrangling and ostentation" of the peri-

patetic philosophy. Yet it was at Oxford
that he encountered the work of Descartes
which first attracted him to metaphysics.
There, too, he met Pocock, the Arabic
scholar, and Wallis the mathematician,
who must at least have commanded his respect. In 1659 he accepted a Senior Stu-
dentship of his college, which he retained
until he was deemed politically undesir-
able in 1684. After toying with his
father's desire that he should enter the
Church, he began the study of medicine.
Scientific interest won for him the friendship of Boyle; and while he was administering physic to the patients of Dr.
Thomas, he was making the observations
recorded in Boyle's *History of the Air*
which Locke himself edited after the
death of his friend.

Meanwhile accident had turned his life
into far different paths. An appointment
as secretary to a special ambassador
opened up to him a diplomatic career; but
his sturdy commonsense showed him his
unfitness for such labors. After his visit
to Prussia he returned to Oxford, and
there, in 1667, in the course of his medical
work, he met Anthony Ashley, the later

Lord Shaftesbury and the Ahitophel of
Dryden's great satire. The two men were
warmly attracted to each other, and
Locke accepted an appointment as phy-
sician to Lord Ashley's household. But
he was also much more than this. The
tutor of Ashley's philosophic grandson, he
became also his patron's confidential coun-
sellor. In 1663 he became part author of
a constitutional scheme for Carolina which
is noteworthy for its emphasis, thus early,
upon the importance of religious toleration. In 1672, when Ashley became Lord
Chancellor, he became Secretary of Pres-
entations and, until 1675, Secretary to the
Council of Trade and Foreign Planta-
tions. Meanwhile he carried on his medical work and must have obtained some
reputation in it; for he is honorably men-
tioned by Sydenham, in his *Method of
Curing Fevers* (1676), and had been
elected to the Royal Society in 1668. But
his real genius lay in other directions.

Locke himself has told us how a few
friends began to meet at his chamber for
the discussions of questions which soon
passed into metaphysical enquiry; and a
page from a commonplace book of 1671

is the first beginning of his systematic
work.   Relieved of his administrative
duties in 1675, he spent the next four
years in France, mainly occupied with
medical observation.   He returned to
England in 1679 to assist Lord Shaftesbury in the passionate debates upon the
Exclusion Bill.   Locke followed his
patron into exile, remaining abroad from
1683 until the Revolution.   Deprived of
his fellowship in 1684 through the malice
of Charles II, he would have been without
means of support had not Shaftesbury be-
queathed him a pension.   As it was, he
had no easy time.   His extradition was
demanded by James II after the Monmouth rebellion; and though he was later
pardoned he refused to return to England
until William of Orange had procured his
freedom.   A year after his return he made
his appearance as a writer.   The *Essay
Concerning Human Understanding* and
the *Two Treatises of Government* were
both published in 1690.   Five years earlier
the *Letter Concerning Toleration* was
published in its Latin dress; and four
years afterwards an English translation
appeared.   This last, however, perhaps on

grounds of expediency, Locke never acknowledged until his will was published;
for the time was not yet suited to such
generous speculations. Locke was thus
in his fifty-eighth year when his first admitted work appeared. But the rough attempts at the essay date from 1671, and
hints towards the *Letter on Toleration*
can be found in fragments of various dates
between the twenty-eighth and thirty-
fifth years of his life. Of the *Two
Treatises* the first seems to have been
written between 1680 and 1685, the
second in the last year of his Dutch exile.[1]

The remaining fourteen years of
Locke's life were passed in semi-retire-
ment in East Anglia. Though he held
public office, first as Commissioner of Ap-
peals, and later of Trade, for twelve years,
he could not stand the pressure of London
writers, and his public work was only in-
termittent. His counsel, nevertheless, was
highly valued; and he seems to have won
no small confidence from William in diplomatic matters. Somers and Charles
Montagu held him in high respect, and he

[1] On the evidence for these dates see the convincing
argument of Mr. Fox-Bourne in his *Life of Locke*,
Vol. II, pp. 165–7.

had the warm friendship of Sir Isaac Newton. He published some short discussions on economic matters, and in 1695 gave valuable assistance in the destruction of the censorship of the press. Two years earlier he had published his *Thoughts on Education,* in which the observant reader may find the germ of most of Emile's ideas. He did not fail to revise the *Essay* from time to time; and his *Reasonableness of Christianity,* which, through Toland, provoked a reply from Stillingfleet and showed Locke in retort a master of the controversial art, was in some sort the foundation of the deistic debate in the next epoch. But his chief work had already been done, and he spent his energies in rewarding the affection of his friends. Locke died on October 28, 1704, amid circumstances of singular majesty. He had lived a full life, and few have so completely realized the medieval ideal of specializing in omniscience. He left warm friends behind him; and Lady Masham has said of him that beyond which no man may dare to aspire.[1]

[1] Fox-Bourne, *op. cit.* Letter from Lady Masham to Jean le Clerc.

III

Locke's *Two Treatises of Government* are different both in object and in value. The first is a detailed and tiresome response to the historic imagination of Sir Robert Filmer. In his *Patriarcha,* which first saw the light in 1680, though it had been written long before, the latter had sought to reach the ultimate conclusion of Hobbes without the element of contract upon which the great thinker depended. "I consent with him," said Filmer of Hobbes, "about the Rights of *exercising* Government, but I cannot agree to his means of acquiring it." That power must be absolute, Filmer, like Hobbes, has no manner of doubt; but his method of proof is to derive the title of Charles I from Adam. Little difficulties like the origin of primogeniture, or whence, as Locke points out, the universal monarchy of Shem can be derived, the good Sir Robert does not satisfactorily determine. Locke takes him up point by point, and there is little enough left, save a sense that history is the root of institutions, when he has done. What troubles us is rather why

Locke should have wasted the resources
of his intelligence upon so feeble an opponent. The book of Hobbes lay ready
to his hand; yet he almost ostentatiously
refused to grapple with it. The answer
doubtless lies in Hobbes' unsavory fame.
The man who made the Church a mere department of the State and justified not
less the title of Cromwell than of the
Stuarts was not the opponent for one who
had a very practical problem in hand.
And Locke could answer that he was answering Hobbes implicitly in the second
Treatise. And though Filmer might
never have been known had not Locke
thus honored him by retort, he doubtless
symbolized what many a nobleman's chaplain preached to his master's dependents
at family prayers.

The *Second Treatise* goes to the root
of the matter. Why does political power,
"a Right of making Laws and Penalties
of Death and consequently all less Penalties," exist? It can only be for the public
benefit, and our enquiry is thus a study of
the grounds of political obedience. Locke
thus traverses the ground Hobbes had
covered in his *Leviathan* though he rejects

every premise of the earlier thinker. To
Hobbes the state of nature which precedes
political organization had been a state of
war. Neither peace nor reason could prevail where every man was his neighbor's
enemy; and the establishment of absolute
power, with the consequent surrender by
men of all their natural liberties, was the
only means of escape from so brutal a régime. That the state of nature was so
distinguished Locke at the outset denies.
The state of nature is governed by the
law of nature. The law of nature is not,
as Hobbes had made it, the antithesis of
real law, but rather its condition antecedent. It is a body of rules which
governs, at all times and all places, the
conduct of men. Its arbiter is reason and,
in the natural state, reason shows us that
men are equal. From this equality are
born men's natural rights which Locke,
like the Independents in the Puritan
Revolution, identifies with life, liberty and
property. Obviously enough, as Hobbes
had also granted, the instinct to self-
preservation is the deepest of human impulses. By liberty Locke means the
right of the individual to follow his own

bent granted only his observance of the law of nature. Law, in such an aspect, is clearly a means to the realization of freedom in the same way that the rule of the road will, by its common acceptance, save its observers from accident. It promotes the initiative of men by defining in terms which by their very statement obtain acknowledgment the conditions upon which individual caprice may have its play. Property Locke derives from a primitive communism which becomes transmuted into individual ownership whenever a man has mingled his labor with some object. This labor theory of ownership lived, it may be remarked, to become, in the hands of Hodgskin and Thompson, the parent of modern socialism.

The state of nature is thus, in contrast to the argument of Hobbes, pre-eminently social in character. There may be war or violence; but that is only when men have abandoned the rule of reason which is integral to their character. But the state of nature is not a civil State. There is no common superior to enforce the law of nature. Each man, as best he may, works out his own interpretation of it. But be-

cause the intelligences of men are different there is an inconvenient variety in
the conceptions of justice. The result is
uncertainty and chaos; and means of escape must be found from a condition
which the weakness of men must ultimately make intolerable. It is here that
the social contract emerges. But just as
Locke's natural state implies a natural
man utterly distinct from Hobbes' gloomy
picture, so does Locke's social contract represent rather the triumph of reason than
of hard necessity. It is a contract of each
with all, a surrender by the individual of
his personal right to fulfil the commands
of the law of nature in return for the
guarantee that his rights as nature ordains
them — life and liberty and property —
will be preserved. The contract is thus
not general as with Hobbes but limited
and specific in character. Nor is it, as
Hobbes made it, the resignation of power
into the hands of some single man or
group. On the contrary, it is a contract
with the community as a whole which thus
becomes that common political superior —
the State — which is to enforce the law of
nature and punish infractions of it. Nor

is Locke's state a sovereign State: the very word "sovereignty" does not occur, significantly enough, throughout the treatise. The State has power only for the protection of natural law. Its province ends when it passes beyond those boundaries.

Such a contract, in Locke's view, involves the pre-eminent necessity of majority-rule. Unless the minority is content to be bound by the will of superior numbers the law of nature has no more protection than it had before the institution of political society. And it is further to be assumed that the individual has surrendered to the community his individual right of carrying out the judgment involved in natural law. Whether Locke conceived the contract so formulated to be historical, it is no easy matter to determine. That no evidence of its early existence can be adduced he ascribes to its origin in the infancy of the race; and the histories of Rome and Sparta and Venice seem to him proof that the theory is somehow demonstrable by facts. More important than origins, he seems to deem its implications. He has placed consent in the foreground of the argument; and he

was anxious to establish the grounds for
its continuance. Can the makers of the
original contract, that is to say, bind their
successors? If legitimate government is
based upon the consent of its subjects,
may they withdraw their consent? And
what of a child born into the community?
Locke is at least logical in his consent.
The contract of obedience must be free or
else, as Hooker had previously insisted, it
is not a contract. Yet Locke urged that
the primitive members of a State are
bound to its perpetuation simply because
unless the majority had power to enforce
obedience government, in any satisfactory
sense, would be impossible. With children the case is different. They are born
subjects of no government or country;
and their consent to its laws must either
be derived from express acknowledgment, or by the tacit implication of the
fact that the protection of the State has
been accepted. But no one is bound until
he has shown by the rule of his mature
conduct that he considers himself a common subject with his fellows. Consent
implies an act of will and we must have
evidence to infer its presence before the
rule of subjection can be applied.

We have thus the State, though the method of its organization is not yet outlined. For Locke there is a difference, though he did not explicitly describe its nature, between State and Government. Indeed he sometimes approximates, without ever formally adopting, the attitude of Pufendorf, his great German contemporary, where government is derived from a secondary contract dependent upon the original institution of civil society. The distinction is made in the light of what is to follow. For Locke was above all anxious to leave supreme power in a community whose single will, as manifested by majority-verdict, could not be challenged by any lesser organ than itself. Government there must be if political society is to endure; but its form and substance are dependent upon popular institution.

Locke follows in the great Aristotelian tradition of dividing the types of government into three. Where the power of making laws is in a single hand we have a monarchy; where it is exercised by a few or all we have alternatively oligarchy and democracy. The disposition of the legislative power is the fundamental test of type; for executive and judiciary are clearly dependent on it. Nor, as Hobbes argued, is the form of government permanent in character; the supreme community is as capable of making temporary as of registering irrevocable decisions. And though Locke admits that monarchy, from its likeness to the family, is the most primitive type of government, he denies Hobbes' assertion that it is the best. It seems, in his view, always to degenerate into the hands of lesser men who betray the contract they were appointed to observe. Nor is oligarchy much better off since it emphasizes the interest of a group against the superior interest of the community as a whole. Democracy alone proffers adequate safeguards of an enduring good rule; a democracy, that is to say, which is in the hands of delegates controlled by popular election. Not that Locke is anxious for the abolition of kingship. His letters show that he disliked the Cromwellian system and the republicanism which Harrington and Milton had based upon it. He was content to have a kingship divested of legislative power so long as hereditary succession was acknowl-

edged to be dependent upon popular consent. The main thing was to be rid of the
Divine Right of kings.

We have thus an organ for the interpretation of natural law free from the shifting variety of individual judgment. We
have a means for securing impartial justice between members of civil society, and
to that means the force of men has been
surrendered. The formulation of the
rules by which life, liberty and property
are to be secured is legislation and this,
from the terms of the original contract, is
the supreme function of the State. But,
in Locke's view, two other functions still
remain. Law has not only to be declared.
It must be enforced; and the business of
the executive is to secure obedience to the
command of law. But Locke here makes
a third distinction. The State must live
with other States, both as regards its individual members, and as a collective
body; and the power which deals with this
aspect of its relationships, Locke termed
"federative." This last distinction, indeed, has no special value; and its author's
own defence of it is far from clear. More
important, especially, for future history,

was his emphasis of the distinction between legislature and executive. The
making of laws is for Locke a relatively
simple and rapid task; the legislature may
do its work and be gone. But those who
attend to their execution must be ceaseless in their vigilance. It is better, therefore, to separate the two both as to powers
and persons. Otherwise legislators "may
exempt themselves from obedience to the
laws they make, and suit the law, both in
its making and its execution, to their own
private wish, and thereby come to have a
distinct interest from the rest of the community, contrary to the end of society and
government." The legislator must therefore be bound by his own laws; and he
must be chosen in such fashion that the
representative assembly may fairly represent its constituencies. It was the patent
anomalies of the existent scheme of distribution which made Locke here proffer
his famous suggestion that the rotten
boroughs should be abolished by executive act. One hundred and forty years
were still to pass before this wise suggestion was translated into statute.

Though Locke thus insisted upon the

separation of powers, he realized that
emergencies are the parent of special
need; and he recognized that not only may
the executive, as in England, share in the
task of legislation, but also may issue ordi-
nances when the legislature is not in session, or act contrary to law in case of
grave danger. Nor can the executive be
forced to summon the legislature. Here,
clearly enough, Locke is generalizing
from the English constitution; and its
sense of compromise is implicit in his remarks. Nor is his surrender here of consent sufficient to be inconsistent with his
general outlook. For at the back of each
governmental act, there is, in his own
mind, an active citizen body occupied in
judging it with single-minded reference
to the law of nature and their own natural
rights. There is thus a standard of right
and wrong superior to all powers within
the State. "A government," as he says, "is
not free to do as it pleases . . . the law
of nature stands as an eternal rule to all
men, legislators as well as others." The
social contract is secreted in the interstices
of public statutes.

Its corollary is the right of revolution.

It is interesting that he should have
adopted this position; for in 1676 he had
uttered the thought that not even the demands of conscience[1] can justify rebellion.
That was, however, before the tyranny of
Charles had driven him into exile with his
patron, and before James had attempted
the subversion of all constitutional government. To deny the right of revolution
was to justify the worst demands of
James, and it is in its favor that he exerts
his ablest controversial power. "The true
remedy," he says, "of force without authority is to oppose force to it." Let the
sovereign but step outside the powers derived from the social contract and resistance becomes a natural right. But how
define such invasion of powers? The instances Locke chose show how closely,
here at least, he was following the events
of 1688. The substitution of arbitrary
will for law, the corruption of Parliament
by packing it with the prince's instruments, betrayal to a foreign prince, prevention of the due assemblage of Parliament — all these are a perversion of the
trust imposed and operate to effect the

[1] King, *Life of Locke*, pp. 62, 63.

dissolution of the contract. The state of nature again supervenes, and a new contract may be made with one more fitted to observe it. Here, also, Locke takes occasion to deny the central position of Hobbes' thesis. Power, the latter had argued, must be absolute and there cannot, therefore, be usurpation. But Locke retorts that an absolute government is no government at all since it proceeds by caprice instead of reason; and it is comparable only to a state of war since it implies the absence of judgment upon the character of power. It lacks the essential element of consent without which the binding force of law is absent. All government is a moral trust, and the idea of limitation is therein implied. But a limitation without the means of enforcement would be worthless, and revolution remains as the reserve power in society. The only hindrance to its exertion that Locke suggests is that of number. Revolution should not, he urges, be the act of a minority; for the contract is the action of the major portion of the people and its consent should likewise obtain to the dissolution of the covenant.

The problem of Church and State demanded a separate discussion; and it is difficult not to feel that the great *Letter on Toleration* is the noblest of all his utterances. It came as the climax to a long evolution of opinion; and, in the light of William's own conviction, it may be said to have marked a decisive epoch of thought. Already in the sixteenth century Robert Brown and William the Silent had denounced the persecution of sincere belief. Early Baptists like Busher and Richardson had finely denied its validity. Roger Williams in America, Milton in England had attacked its moral rightness and political adequacy; while churchmen like Hales and Taylor and the noble Chillingworth had shown the incompatibility between a religion of love and a spirit of hate. Nor had example been wanting. The religious freedom of Holland was narrow, as Spinoza had found, but it was still freedom. Rhode Island, Pennsylvania, South Carolina and Massachusetts had all embarked upon admirable experiment; and Penn himself had aptly said that a man may go to chapel instead of church, even while he remains

a good constable.   And in 1687, in the
preface to his translation of Lactantius,
Burnet had not merely attacked the moral
viciousness of persecution, but had drawn
a distinction between the spheres of
Church and State which is a remarkable
anticipation of Locke's own theory.

Locke himself covers the whole ground;
and since his opinions on the problem were
at least twenty years old, it is clear that
he was consistent in a worthy outlook. He
proceeds by a denial that any element of
theocratic government can claim political
validity. The magistrate is concerned
only with the preservation of social peace
and does not deal with the problem of
men's souls. Where, indeed, opinions destructive of the State are entertained or a
party subversive of peace makes its appearance, the magistrate has the right of
suppression; though in the latter case
force is the worst and last of remedies. In
the English situation, it follows that all
men are to be tolerated save Catholics,
Mahomedans and atheists. The first are
themselves deniers of the rights they
would seek, and they find the centre of
their political allegiance in a foreign

power.   Mahomedan morals are incompatible with European civil systems; and the central factor in atheism is the absence of the only ultimately satisfactory sanction of good conduct.   Though Church and State are thus distinct, they act for a reciprocal benefit; and it is thus important to see why Locke insists on the invalidity of persecution.   For such an end as the cure of souls, he argues, the magistrate has no divine legation.   He cannot, on other grounds, use force for the simple reason that it does not produce internal conviction.   But even if that were possible, force would still be mistaken; for the majority of the world is not Christian, yet it would have the right to persecute in the belief that it was possessed of truth.   Nor can the implication that the magistrate has the keys of heaven be accepted.   "No religion," says Locke finely, "which I believe not to be true can be either true or profitable to me."   He thus makes of the Church an institution radically different from the ruling conceptions of his time. It becomes merely a voluntary society, which can exert no power save over its members.   It may use its own ceremonies, but it cannot impose them on the unwilling; and since persecution is alien from the spirit of Christ, exclusion from membership must be the limit of ecclesiastical disciplinary power. Nor must we forget the advantages of toleration. Its eldest child is charity, and without it there can be no honesty of opinion. Later controversy did not make him modify these principles; and they lived, in Macaulay's hands, to be a vital weapon in the political method of the nineteenth century.

IV

Any survey of earlier political theory would show how little of novelty there is in the specific elements of Locke's general doctrine. He is at all points the offspring of a great and unbroken tradition; and that not the least when he seems unconscious of it. Definite teachers, indeed, he can hardly be said to have had; no one can read his book without perceiving how much of it is rooted in the problems of his own day. He himself has expressed his sense of Hooker's greatness, and he elsewhere had recommended the works of

Grotius and Pufendorf as an essential element in education. But his was a nature
which learned more from men than
books; and he more than once insisted that
his philosophy was woven of his own
"coarse thoughts." What, doubtless, he
therein meant was to emphasize the fresh-
ness of his contact with contemporary
fact in contrast with the technical jargon
of the earlier thinkers. At least his work
is free from the mountains of allusion
which Prynne rolled into the bottom of
his pages; and if the first Whig was the
devil, he is singularly free from the irritating pedantry of biblical citation. Yet
even with these novelties, no estimate of
his work would be complete which failed
to take account of the foundations upon
which he builded.

Herein, perhaps, the danger is lest we
exaggerate Locke's dependence upon the
earlier current of thought. The social
contract is at least as old as when Glaucon
debated with Socrates in the market-place
at Athens. The theory of a state of
nature, with the rights therein implied, is
the contribution, through Stoicism, of the
Roman lawyers, and the great medieval

contrast to Aristotle's experimentalism.
To the latter, also, may be traced the separation of powers; and it was then but
little more than a hundred years since
Bodin had been taken to make the doctrine an integral part of scientific politics.
Nor is the theory of a right to revolution
in any sense his specific creation. So
soon as the Reformation had given a new
perspective to the problem of Church and
State every element of Locke's doctrine
had become a commonplace of debate.
Goodman and Knox among Presbyterians, Suarez and Mariana among
Catholics, the author of the *Vindiciæ* and
Francis Hotman among the Huguenots,
had all of them emphasized the concept of
public power as a trust; with, of course,
the necessary corollary that its abuse en-
tails resistance. Algernon Sydney was at
least his acquaintance; and he must have
been acquainted with the tradition, even
if tragedy spared him the details, of the
Discourses on Government. Even his
theory of toleration had in every detail
been anticipated by one or other of a hundred controversialists; and his argument
can hardly claim either the lofty eloquence

of Jeremy Taylor or the cogent simplicity
of William Penn.

What differentiates Locke from all his
predecessors is the manner of his writing
on the one hand, and the fact of the Revolution on the other. Every previous
thinker save Sydney — the latter's work
was not published until 1689 — was writing with the Church hardly less in mind
than the purely political problems of the
State; even the secular Hobbes had devoted much thought and space to that
"kingdom of darkness" which is Rome.
And, Sydney apart, the resistance they
had justified was always resistance to a religious tyrant; and Cartwright was as
careful to exclude political oppression
from the grounds of revolution as Locke
was to insist upon it as the fundamental
excuse. Locke is, in fact, the first of English thinkers the basis of whose argument
is mainly secular. Not, indeed, that he can
wholly escape the trammels of ecclesias-
ticism; not until the sceptical intelligence
of Hume was such freedom possible. But
it is clear enough that Locke was shifting
to very different ground from that which
arrested the attention of his predecessors.

He is attempting, that is to say, a separation between Church and State not merely in that Scoto-Jesuit sense which aimed at ecclesiastical independence, but in order to assert the pre-eminence of the State as such. The central problem is with him political, and all other questions are subsidiary to it. Therein we have a sense, less clear in any previous writer save Machiavelli, of the real result of the decay of medieval ideals. Church and State have become transposed in their significance. The way, as a consequence, lies open to new dogmas.

The historical research of the nineteenth century has long since made an end of the social contract as an explanation of state-origins; and with it, of necessity, has gone the conception of natural rights as anterior to organized society. The problem, as we now know, is far more complex than the older thinkers imagined. Yet Locke's insistence on consent and natural rights has received new meaning from each critical period of history since he wrote. The theory of consent is vital because without the provision of channels for its administrative expression, men tend to become the creatures of a power ignorant at once and careless of their will. Active consent on the part of the mass of men emphasizes the contingent nature of all power and is essential to the full realization of freedom; and the purpose of the State, in any sense save the mere satisfaction of material appetite, remains, without it, unfulfilled. The concept of natural right is most closely related to this position. For so long as we regard rights as no more than the creatures of law, there is at no point adequate safeguard against their usurpation. A merely legal theory of the State can never, therefore, exhaust the problems of political philosophy.

No thinker has seen this fact more clearly than Locke; and if his effort to make rights something more than interests under juridical protection can not be accepted in the form he made it, the underlying purpose remains. A State, that is to say, which aims at giving to men the full capacity their trained initiative would permit is compelled to regard certain things as beyond the action of an ordinary legislature. What Stammler calls a "nat-

ural law with changing content"[1] — a
content which changes with our increasing
power to satisfy demand — is essential if
the state is to live the life of law. For
here was the head and centre of Locke's
enquiry. "What he was really concerned
about," said T. H. Green, "was to dispute 'the right divine of kings to govern
wrong.'" The method, as he conceived,
by which this could be accomplished was
the limitation of power. This he effected
by two distinct methods, the one external,
the other internal, in character.

The external method has, at bottom,
two sides. It is, in the first place, achieved
by a narrow definition of the purpose of
the state. To Locke the State is little
more than a negative institution, a kind of
gigantic limited liability company; and if
we are inclined to cavil at such restraint,
we may perhaps remember that even to
neo-Hegelians like Green and Bosanquet
this negative sense is rarely absent, in the
interest of individual exertion. But for
Locke the real guarantee of right lies in
another direction. What his whole work

[1] Cf. my *Authority in the Modern State,* p. 64., and
the references there cited.

amounts to in substance — it is a significant anticipation of Rousseau — is a
denial that sovereignty can exist anywhere
save in the community as a whole. A common political superior there doubtless
must be; but government is an organ to
which omnipotence is wanting. So far as
there is a sovereign at all in Locke's book,
it is the will of that majority which Rousseau tried to disguise under the name of
the general will; but obviously the conception lacks precision enough to give the notion of sovereignty the means of operation.
The denial is natural enough to a man who
had seen, under three sovereigns, the evils
of unlimited power; and if there is lacking
to his doctrine the well-rounded logic of
Hobbes' proof that an unlimited sovereign
is unavoidable, it is well to remember that
the shift of opinion is, in our own time,
more and more in the direction of Locke's
attitude. That omnicompetence of Parliament which Bentham and Austin crys-
tallized into the retort to Locke admits, in
later hands, of exactly the amelioration he
had in mind; and its ethical inadequacy
becomes the more obvious the more closely
it is studied.[1]

[1] Cf. my *Problem of Sovereignty*, Chap. I.

The internal limitation Locke suggested is of more doubtful value. Government, he says, in substance, is a trustee and trustees abuse their power; let us therefore divide it as to parts and persons that the temptation to usurp may be diminished. There is a long history to this doctrine in its more obvious form, and it is a lamentable history. It tied men down to a tyrannous classification which had no root in the material it was supposed to distinguish. Montesquieu took it for the root of liberty; Blackstone, who should have known better, repeated the pious phrases of the Frenchman; and they went in company to America to persuade Madison and the Supreme Court of the United States that only the separation of powers can prevent the approach of tyranny. The facts do not bear out such assumption. The division of powers means in the event not less than their confusion. None can differentiate between the judge's declaration of law and his making of it.[1] Every government department is compelled to legislate, and, often enough, to undertake

[1] Cf. Mr. Justice Holmes' remarks in *Jensen* v. *Southern Pacific*, 244 U. S. 221.

judicial functions. The American history
of the separation of powers has most
largely been an attempt to bridge them;
and all that has been gained is to drive the
best talent, save on rare occasion, from its
public life. In France the separation of
powers meant, until recent times, the ex-
cessive subordination of the judiciary to
the cabinet. Nor must we forget, as
Locke should have remembered, the plain
lesson of the Cromwellian constitutional
experiments. That the dispersion of power
is one of the great needs of the modern
State at no point justifies the rigid categories into which Locke sought its
division.[1]

Nor must we belittle the criticism, in its
clearest form the work of Fitz James
Stephen,[2] that has been levelled at Locke's
theory of toleration. For the larger part
of the modern world, his argument is acceptable enough; and its ingenious com-
promises have made it especially representative of the English temper. Yet much
of it hardly meets the argument that some
of his opponents, as Proast for example,

[1] Cf. my *Authority in the Modern State*, pp. 70 f.
[2] Cf. also Coleridge's apt remark. *Table Talk*, Jan.
3, 1834.

had made. His conception of the visible church as no part of the essence of religion could win no assent from even a moderate Anglican; and, once the visible church is admitted, Locke's facile distinction between Church and State falls to the ground. Nor can it be doubted that he underestimated the power of coercion to produce assent; the policy of Louis XIV to the Huguenots may have been brutal, but its efficacy must be unquestionable. And it is at least doubtful whether his theory has any validity for a man who held, as Roman Catholics of his generation were bound to hold, that the communication of his particular brand of truth outweighed in value all other questions. "Every Church," he wrote, "is orthodox to itself; to others, erroneous or heretical"; but to any earnest believer this would approximate to blasphemy. Nor could any serious Christian accept the view that "under the gospel '. . . there is no such thing as a Christian commonwealth' "; to Catholics and Presbyterians this must have appeared the merest travesty of their faith.

Here, indeed, as elsewhere Locke is the

true progenitor of Benthamism, and his
work can hardly be understood save in this
context. Just as in his ethical enquiries
it was always the happiness of the individual that he sought, so in his politics it
was the happiness of the subject he had in
view. In each case it was to immediate experience that he made his appeal; and this
perhaps explains the clear sense of a contempt for past tradition which pervades
all his work. "That which is for the public welfare," he said, "is God's will"; and
therein we have the root of that utilitarianism which, as Maine pointed out, is the
real parent of all nineteenth century
change. And with Locke, as with the
Benthamites, his clear sense of what utilitarianism demanded led to an over-emphasis of human rationalism. No one can read
the *Second Treatise* without perceiving
that Locke looked upon the State as a machine which can be built and taken to
pieces in very simple fashion. Herein, undoubtedly, he over-simplified the problem;
and that made him miss some of the cardi-
nal points a true psychology of the State
must seize. His very contractualism, indeed, is part of this affection for the ra-

tional. It resulted in his failure to perceive how complex is the mass of motives
imbedded in the political act. The significance of herd instinct and the vast primitive deeps of the unconscious were alike
hidden from him. All this is of defect;
and yet excusably. For it needed the
demonstration by Darwin of the kinship
of man and beast for us to see the real substance of Aristotle's vision that man is
embedded in political society.

V

Once Locke's work had become known,
its reputation was secure. Not, indeed,
that it was entirely welcome to his generation. Men were not wanting who shrank
from his thoroughgoing rationalism and
felt that anything but reason must be the
test of truth. Those who stood by the
ancient ways found it easy to discover republicanism and the roots of atheistic doctrine in his work; and even the theories of
Filmer could find defenders against him
in the Indian summer of prerogative under Queen Anne. John Hutton informed
a friend that he was not less dangerous

than Spinoza; and the opinion found an
echo from the nonjuring sect. But these,
after all, were but the eddies of a stream
fast burying itself in the sands. For most,
the Revolution was a final settlement, and
Locke was welcome as a writer who had
discovered the true source of political
comfort. So it was that William Molyneux could embody the ideas of the "incomparable treatise" in his demand for
Irish freedom; a book which, even in those
days, occasioned some controversy. Nor
is it uninteresting to discover that the
translation of Hotman's *Franco-Gallia*
should have been embellished with a preface from one who, as Molyneux wrote to
Locke,[1] never met the Irish writer without conversing of their common master.
How rapidly the doctrine spread we learn
from a letter of Bayle's in which, as early
as 1693, Locke has already became "the
gospel of the Protestants." Nor was his
immediate influence confined to England.
French Huguenots and the Dutch drew
naturally upon so happy a defender; and
Barbeyrac, in the translation of Pufendorf which he published in 1706, cites no

[1] Locke, Works (ed. of 1812), IX. 435.

writer so often as Locke. The speeches
for the prosecution in the trial of Sacheverell were almost wholesale adaptations
of his teaching; and even the accused counsel admitted the legality of James' deposition in his speech for the defence.

More valuable testimony is not wanting.
In the *Spectator,* on six separate occa-
sions, Addison speaks of him as one whose
possession is a national glory. Defoe in
his *Original Power of the People of England* made Locke the common possession
of the average man, and offered his ac-
knowledgments to his master. Even the
malignant genius of Swift softened his
hate to find the epithet "judicious" for
one in whose doctrines he can have found
no comfort. Pope summarized his teaching in the form that Bolingbroke chose
to give it. Hoadly, in his *Original and Institution of Civil Government,* not only
dismisses Filmer in a first part each page
of which is modelled upon Locke, but
adds a second section in which a defence of
Hooker serves rather clumsily to conceal
the care with which the *Second Treatise*
had also been pillaged. Even Warburton
ceased for a moment his habit of belittling

all rivals in the field he considered his own
to call him, in that *Divine Legation* which
he considered his masterpiece, "the honor
of this age and the instructor of the
future"; but since Warburton's attack on
the High Church theory is at every point
Locke's argument, he may have considered this self-eulogy instead of tribute.
Sir Thomas Hollis, on the eve of English
Radicalism, published a noble edition of
his book.   And there is perhaps a certain
humor in the remembrance that it was to
Locke's economic tracts that Bolingbroke
went for the arguments with which, in the
Craftsman, he attacked the excise scheme
of Walpole.   That is irrefutable evidence
of the position he had attained.

Yet the tide was already on the ebb, and
for cogent reasons.   There still remained
the tribute to be paid by Montesquieu
when he made Locke's separation of
powers the keystone of his own more
splendid arch.   The most splendid of all
sciolists was still to use his book for the
outline of a social contract more daring
even than his own.   The authors of the
Declaration of Independence had still, in
words taken from Locke, to reassert the

state of nature and his rights; and Mr.
Martin of North Carolina was to find him
quotable in the debates of the Philadelphia
Convention.   Yet Locke's own weapons
were being turned against him and what
was permanent in his work was being cast
into the new form required by the time.
A few sentences of Hume were sufficient
to make the social contract as worthless as
the Divine Right of kings, and when
Blackstone came to sum up the result of
the Revolution, if he wrote in contractual
terms it was with a full admission that he
was making use of fiction so far as he went
behind the settlement of 1688.   Nor is the
work of Dean Tucker without significance.   The failure of England in the
American war was already evident; and it
was not without justice that he looked
to Locke as the author of their principles.
"The Americans," he wrote, "have made
the maxims of Locke the ground of the
present war"; and in his *Treatise Concerning Civil Government* and his
Four Letters he declares himself unable to
understand on what Locke's reputation
was based.   Meanwhile the English disciples of Rousseau in the persons of Price

and Priestley suggested to him that
Locke, "the idol of the levellers of England," was the parent also of French de-
structiveness. Burke took up the work
thus begun; and after he had dealt with
the contract theory it ceased to influence
political speculation in England. Its
place was taken by the utilitarian doctrine
which Hume had outlined; and once
Bentham's *Fragment* had begun to make
its way, a new epoch opened in the history
of political ideas.

Locke might, indeed, claim that he had
a part in this renaissance; but, once the
influence of Burke had passed, it was to
other gods men turned. For Bentham
made an end of natural rights; and his
contempt for the past was even more unsparing than Locke's own. It is more
instructive to compare his work with
Hobbes and Rousseau than with later
thinkers; for after Hume English speculation works in a medium Locke would
not have understood. Clearly enough, he
has nothing of the relentless logic which
made Hobbes' mind the clearest instrument in the history of English philosophy.
Nor has he Hobbes' sense of style or pun-

gent grasp of the grimness of facts about
him. Yet he need not fear the comparison
with the earlier thinker. If Hobbes'
theory of sovereignty is today one of the
commonplaces of jurisprudence, ethically
and politically we occupy ourselves with
erecting about it a system of limitations
each one of which is in some sort due to
Locke's perception. If we reject Locke's
view of the natural goodness of men,
Hobbes' sense of their evil character is
not less remote from our speculations.
Nor can we accept Hobbes' Erastianism.
Locke's view of Church and State became,
indeed, a kind of stepchild to it in the
stagnant days of the later Georges; but
Wesleyanism, on the one hand, and the
Oxford movement on the other, pointed
the inevitable moral of even an approxi-
mation to the Hobbesian view. And anyone who surveys the history of Church and
State in America will be tempted to assert
that in the last hundred years the sepa-
rateness for which Locke contended is not
without its justification. Locke's theory
is a means of preserving the humanity of
men; Hobbes makes their reason and conscience the subjects of a power he forbids

them to judge. Locke saw that vigilance
is the sister of liberty, where Hobbes dismissed the one as faction and the other as
disorder. At every point, that is to say,
where Hobbes and Locke are at variance,
the future has been on Locke's side. He
may have defended his cause less splendidly than his rival; but it will at least be
admitted by most that he had a more
splendid cause to defend.

With Rousseau there is no con-
trast, for the simple reason that his teaching is only a broadening of the channel
dug by Locke. No element integral to
the *Two Treatises* is absent from the *Social Contract*. Rousseau, indeed, in many
aspects saw deeper than his predecessor.
The form into which he threw his questions gave them an eternal significance
Locke can perhaps hardly claim. He
understood the organic character of the
State, where Locke was still trammelled
by the bonds of his narrow individualism.
It is yet difficult to see that the contribution upon which Rousseau's fame has
mainly rested is at any point a real advance upon Locke. The general will, in
practical instead of semi-mystic terms,

really means the welfare of the community as a whole; and when we enquire how that general will is to be known, we come, after much shuffling, upon the will of that majority in which Locke also put his trust. Rousseau's general will, indeed, is at bottom no more than an assertion that right and truth should prevail; and for this also Locke was anxious. But he did not think an infallible criterion existed for its detection; and he was satisfied with the convenience of a simple numerical test. Nor would it be difficult to show that Locke's state has more real room for individuality than Rousseau's. The latter made much show of an impartible and inalienable sovereignty eternally vested in the people; but in practice its exercise is impossible outside the confines of a city-state. Once, that is to say, we deal with modern problems our real enquiry is still the question of Locke — what limits shall we place upon the power of government? Rousseau has only emphasized the urgency of the debate.

Wherein, perhaps, the most profound distinction between Locke's teaching and our own time may be discovered is in our

sense of the impossibility that a final answer can be found to political questions.
Each age has new materials at its command; and, today, a static philosophy
would condemn itself before completion.
We do not build Utopias; and the attempt
to discover the eternal principles of political right invites disaster at the outset.
Yet that does not render useless, even for
our own day, the kind of work Locke did.
In the largest sense, his questions are still
our own. In the largest sense, also, we
are near enough to his time to profit at
each step of our own efforts by the hints
he proffers. The point at which he stood
in English history bears not a little re-
semblance to our own. The emphasis, now
as then, is upon the problem of freedom.
The problem, now as then, was its translation into institutional terms. It is the
glory of Locke that he brought a generous
patience and a searching wisdom to the solution he proffered to his generation.

CHAPTER III

I

THE Revolution of 1688 drew its main
source of strength from the traditional
dislike of Rome, and the eager desire to
place the Church of England beyond the
reach of James' aggression. Yet it was
not until a generation had passed that the
lines of ecclesiastical settlement were, in
any full sense clear. The difficulties involved were mostly governmental, and it
can hardly even yet be said that they have
been solved. The nature of the relation
between Church and State, the affiliation
between the Church and Nonconformist
bodies, the character of its internal government — all these had still to be defined.
Nor was this all. The problem of definition was made more complex by schism
and disloyalty. An important fraction of

the Church could not accept at all the fact
of William's kingship; and if the larger
part submitted, it cannot be said to have
been enthusiastic.

Nor did the Church make easy the situation of the Nonconformists. Toleration
of some kind was rapidly becoming inevitable; and with a Calvinist upon the
throne persecution of, at any rate, the
Presbyterians became finally impossible.
Yet the definition of what limits were to
be set to toleration was far from easy.
The Church seemed like a fortress be-
leaguered when Nonjurors, Deists, Nonconformists, all alike assaulted her foundations. To loosen her hold upon political
privilege seemed to be akin to self-destruc-
tion. And, after all, if Church and State
were to stand in some connection, the
former must have some benefit from the
alliance. Did such partnership imply exclusion from its privilege for all who could
not accept the special brand of religious
doctrine? Locke, at least, denied the assumption, and argued that since Churches
are voluntary societies, they cannot and
ought not to have reciprocal relation with
the State. But Locke's theory was meat

too strong for the digestion of his time;
and no statesman would then have argued
that a government could forego the ad-
vantage of religious support. And
William, after all, had come to free the
church from her oppressor. Freedom implied protection, and protection in that
age involved establishment. It was thus
taken for granted by most members of the
Church of England that her adoption by
the State meant her superiority to every
other form of religious organization. Superiority is, by its nature exclusive, the
more especially when it is united to a certainty of truth and a kinship with the
dominant political interest of the time.
Long years were thus to pass before the
real meaning of the Toleration Act secured translation into more generous
statutes.

The problem of the Church's government was hardly less complex. The very
acerbity with which it was discussed proclaims that we are in an age of settlement.
Much of the dispute, indeed, is doubtless
due to the dislike of all High Churchmen
for William; with their consequent unwillingness to admit the full meaning of

his ecclesiastical supremacy.   Much also
is due to the fact that the bench of bishops,
despite great figures like Tillotson and
Wake, was necessarily chosen for political
aptitude rather than for religious value.
Nor did men like Burnet and Hoadly, for
all their learning, make easy the path for
brethren of more tender consciences. The
Church, moreover, must have felt its
powers the more valuable from the very
strength of the assault to which she was
subjected. And the direct interference
with her governance implied by the Oaths
of Allegiance and of Abjuration raised
questions we have not yet solved. It suggested the subordination of Church to
State; and men like Hickes and Leslie
were quick to point out the Erastianism of
the age. It is a fact inevitable in the situation of the English Church that the
charge of subjection to the State should
rouse a deep and quick resentment. She
cannot be a church unless she is a *societas
perfecta;* she cannot have within herself
the elements of perfect fellowship if what
seem the plain commands of Christ are to
be at the mercy of the king in Parliament. That is the difficulty which lies at

the bottom of the debate with Wake in one age and with Hoadly in the next. In some sort, it is the problem of sovereignty that is here at issue; and it is in this sense that the problems of the Revolution are linked with the Oxford Movement. But Newman and his followers are the unconscious sponsors of a debate which grows in volume; and to discuss the thoughts of Wake and Hoadly and Law is thus, in a vital aspect, the study of contemporary ideas.

We are not here concerned with the wisdom of those of William's advisers who exacted an oath of allegiance from the clergy. It raised in acute form the validity of a doctrine which had, for more than a century, been the main foundation of the alliance between throne and altar in England. The demand precipitated a schism which lingered on, though fitfully, until the threshold of the nineteenth century. The men who could not take the oath were, many of them, among the most distinguished churchmen of the time. Great ecclesiastics like Sancroft, the archbishop of Canterbury and one of the seven who had gained immortality by his resistance to James, saints like Ken, the bishop of Bath and Wells, scholars like George Hickes and Henry Dodwell, men like Charles Leslie, born with a genius for recrimination; much, it is clear, of what was best in the Church of England was to be found amongst them. There is not a little of beauty, and much of pathos in their history. Most, after their deprivation, were condemned to poverty; few of them recanted. The lives of men like Sancroft and Ken and the younger Ambrose Bonwicke are part of the great Anglican tradition of earnest simplicity which later John Keble was to illustrate for the nineteenth century. The Nonjurors, as they were called, were not free from bitterness; and the history of their effort, after the consecration of Hilkiah Bedford and Ralph Taylor, to perpetuate the schism is a lamentable one. Not, indeed, that the history even of their decline is without its interest; and the study, alike of their liturgy and their attempt at reunion with the Eastern Church, must always possess a singular interest for students of ecclesiastical history.

Yet the real interest of the Nonjuring

schism was political rather than religious;
and its roots go out to vital events of the
past. At the bottom it is the obverse side
of the Divine Right of kings that they
represent. That theory, which was the
main weapon of the early secular state
against the pretensions of Rome, must
naturally have commanded the allegiance
of members of a church which James I,
its main exponent, had declared of vital
import to his very existence. Its main
opponents, moreover, were Catholics and
Dissenters; so that men like Andrewes
must have felt that when they answered
Bellarmine they were in substance also defenders of their Church. After the great
controversy of James I's reign resistance
as a duty had come to be regarded as a
main element in Jesuit and Nonconformist teaching; with the result that its
antithesis became, as a consequence of the
political situation, no less integral a part
of Church of England doctrine. For it
was upon the monarchy that the Church
had come to depend for its existence; and
if resistance to the king were made, as
Knox and Bellarmine had in substance
made it, the main weapon of the dissent-

ing churches there was little hope that it
would continue to exist once the monarchy
was overthrown. And it is this, unquestionably, which explains why stout ecclesiastics like Barrow and Jackson can
write in what seems so Erastian a temper.
When they urge the sovereignty of the
State, their thesis is in truth the sovereignty of the Church; and that means
the triumph of men who looked with contemptuous hatred upon Nonconformists
of every sect. The Church of England
taught non-resistance as the condition of
its own survival.

How deep-rooted this doctrine had become in the course of the seventeenth century the writings of men like Mainwaring
and Sanderson sufficiently show; yet
nothing so completely demonstrates its
widespread acceptance as the result of
the Revolution. Four hundred clergy
abandoned their preferment because
James ruled by Divine Right; and they
could not in conscience resist even his iniquities. An able tract of 1689[1] had collected much material to show how in-

---

[1] *The History of Passive Obedience.* Its author was
Jeremy Collier.

tegral the doctrine was to the beliefs of the
Church. Had William's government, indeed, refrained from the imposition of
the oath, it is possible that there might
have been no schism at all; for the early
Nonjurors at least — perhaps Hickes and
Turner are exceptions — would probably
have welcomed anything which enabled
the avoidance of schism. Once, however,
the oath was imposed three vital questions
were raised. Deprivation obviously involved the problem of the power of the
State over the Church. If the act of a convention whose own legality was at best
doubtful could deprive the consecrated of
their position, was the Church a Church at
all, or was it the mere creature of the
secular power? And what, moreover, of
conscience? It could not be an inherent
part of the Church's belief that men
should betray their faith for the sake of
peace. Later thinkers added the purely
secular argument that resistance in one
case made for resistance in all. Admit,
it was argued by Leslie, the right to disobey, and the fabric of society is at a
stroke dissolved. The attitude is characteristic of that able controversialist; and

it shows how hardly the earlier notions of
Divine Right were to die.

These theories merit a further examination. Williams, later the Bishop of
Chichester, had argued that separation on
the basis of the oath was unreasonable.
"All that the civil power here pretends
to," he wrote "is to secure itself against
the practices of dissatisfied persons." The
Nonjurors, in this view, were making an
ecclesiastical matter of a purely secular
issue. He was answered, among others,
by Samuel Grascom, in an argument
which found high favor among the stricter
of his sect. "The matter and substance of
these Oaths," he said, "is put into the
prayers of the Church, and so far it becomes a matter of communion. What
people are enjoined in the solemn worship
to pray for, is made a matter of communion; and if it be simple, will not only
justify, but require a separation." Here
is the pith of the matter. For if the form
and substance of Church affairs is thus to
be left to governmental will, then those
who obey have left the Church and it is
the faithful remnant only who constitute
the true fellowship. The schism, in this

view, was the fault of those who remained
subject to William's dominion. The Nonjurors had not changed; and they were
preserving the Church in its integrity
from men who strove to betray it to the
civil power.

This matter of integrity is important.
The glamour of Macaulay has somewhat
softened the situation of those who took
the oaths; and in his pages the Nonjurors
appear as stupid men unworthily defend-
ing a dead cause. It is worth while to note
that this is the merest travesty. Tillotson, who succeeded Sancroft on the latter's
deprivation, and Burnet himself had
urged passive resistance upon Lord
William Russell as essential to salvation;
Tenison had done likewise at the execution of Monmouth. Stillingfleet, Patrick,
White Kennett, had all written in its
favor; and to William Sherlock belongs
the privilege of having defended and attacked it in two pamphlets each of which
challenges the pithy brilliance of the other.
Clearly, so far as consistency is in question, the Nonjurors might with justice
contend that they had right on their side.
And even if it is said that the policy of

James introduced a new situation the answer surely is that Divine Right and non-resistance can, by their very nature, make no allowance for novelty.

The root, then, of this ecclesiastical contention is the argument later advanced by Leslie in his "Case of the Regale and the Pontificate" in which he summarized the Convocation dispute. The State, he argues, has no power over bishops whose relationship to their flock is purely spiritual and derived from Christ. The Church is independent of all civil institution, and must have therefore within herself the powers necessary to her life as a society. Leslie repudiates Erastianism in the strongest terms. Not only is it, for him, an encroachment upon the rights of Christ, but it leads to deism in the gentry and to dissent among the common people. The Church of England comes to be regarded as no more than the creature of Parliamentary enactment; and thus to leave it as the creature of human votes, is to destroy its divinity.

It is easy enough to see that men who felt in this fashion could hardly have decided otherwise than as they did. The

matter of conscience, indeed, was fundamental to their position. "I think," said
the Bishop of Worcester on his death-bed,
"I could suffer at a stake rather than
take this oath." That, indeed, represents
the general temper. Many of them did
not doubt that James had done grievous
wrong; but they had taken the oath of allegiance to him, and they saw in their conscience no means of escape from their
vow. "Their Majesties," writes the
author of the account of Bishop Lake's
death, "are the two persons in the world
whose reign over them, their interest and
inclination oblige them most to desire, and
nothing but conscience could restrain them
from being as forward as any in all ex-
pressions of loyalty." In such an aspect,
even those who believe their attitude to
have been wrong, can hardly doubt that
they acted rightly in their expression of
it. For, after all, experience has shown
that the State is built upon the consciences
of men. And the protest they made
stands out in the next generation in vivid
contrast to a worldly-minded and politi-
cally-corrupt Church which only internal
revolution could awaken from its slum-
bers.

No one represents so admirably as
Charles Leslie the political argument of
the case. At bottom it is an argument
against anarchy that he constructs, and
much of what he said is medieval enough
in tone to suggest de Maistre's great defence of papalism as the secret of world-
order. He stands four square upon
divine right and passive obedience.
"What man is he who can by his own natural authority bend the conscience of another? That would be far more than the
power of life, liberty or prosperity.
Therefore they saw the necessity of a
divine original." Such a foundation, he
argued elsewhere, is necessary to order,
for "if the last resort be in the people,
there is no end of controversy at all, but
endless and unremediable confusion."
Nor had he sympathy for the Whig attack on monarchy. "The reasons against
Kings," he wrote, "are as strong against
all powers, for men of any titles are subject to err, and numbers more than
fewer." And nothing can unloose the
chain. "Obedience," he said in the *Best
of All,* "is due to commonwealths by their
subjects even for conscience' sake, where

the princes from whom they have revolted
have given up their claim."

The argument has a wider history than
its controversial statement might seem to
warrant. At bottom, clearly enough, it
is an attack upon the new tradition which
Locke had brought into being. What
seems to impress it most is the impossibility of founding society upon other than
a divine origin. Anything less will not
command the assent of men sufficiently to
be immune from their evil passions. Let
their minds but once turn to resistance, and
the bonds of social order will be broken.
Complete submission is the only safeguard
against anarchy. So, a century later, de
Maistre could argue that unless the whole
world became the subject of Rome, the
complete dissolution of Christian society
must follow. So, too, fifty years before,
Hobbes had argued for an absolute dominion lest the ambitions and desires of
men break through the fragile boundaries
of the social estate.

The answer is clear enough; and, indeed, the case against the Nonjurors is
nowhere so strong as on its political side.
Men cannot be confined within the limits

of so narrow a logic. They will not, with
Bishop Ken, rejoice in suffering as a doctrine of the Cross. Rather will oppression
in its turn arouse a sense of wrong and
that be parent of a conscience which provokes to action. Here was the root of
Locke's doctrine of consent; for unless the
government, as Hume was later to point
out, has on its side the opinion of men, it
cannot hope to endure. The fall of James
was caused, not as the Nonjurors were
tempted to think, by popular disregard of
Divine personality, but by his own mis-
understanding of the limits to which mis-
government may go. Here their opponents had a strong case to present; for,
as Stillingfleet remarked, if William had
not come over there might have been no
Church of England for the Nonjurors to
preserve. And other ingenious compro-
mises were suggested. Non-resistance, it
was argued by Sherlock, applied to government in general; and the oath, as a
passage in the *Convocation Book* of Over-
all seemed to suggest, might be taken not
less to a *de facto* monarch than to one *de
jure*. Few, indeed would have taken the
ground of Bishop Burnet, and allotted the

throne to William and Mary as con-
querors of the Kingdom; at least the
pamphlet in which this uncomfortable
doctrine was put forward the House of
Commons had burned by the common
hangman.

What really defeated the Nonjurors'
claims was commonsense. Much the
ablest attack upon their position was Stillingfleet's defence of the policy employed
in filling up the sees vacated by deprivation; and it is remarkable that the theory
he employs is to insist that unless the law-
fulness of what had been done is admitted,
the Nonjuror's position is inevitable. "If
it be unlawful to succeed a deprived
bishop," he wrote,[1] "then he is the bishop
of the diocese still: and then the law that
deprives him is no law, and consequently
the king and Parliament that made that
law no king and Parliament: and how can
this be reconciled with the Oath of Allegiance, unless the Doctor can swear allegiance to him who is no King and hath
no authority to govern." All this the
Nonjurors would have admitted, and the

[1] *A Vindication of their Majesties' Authority to fill
the Sees of the Deprived Bishops* (1691).

mere fact that it could be used as argument against them is proof that they were out of touch with the national temper. What they wanted was a legal revolution which is in the nature of things impossible. We may regret that the oath was deemed essential, and feel that it might not have been so stoutly pressed. But the leaders of a revolution "tread a path of fire"; and the fault lay less at the door of the civil government than in the fact that this was an age when men acted on their principles. William and his advisers, with the condition of Ireland and Scotland a cause for agitation, with France hostile, with treason and plot not absent from the episcopate itself, had no easy task; what, in the temper of the time, gives most cause for consideration, is the moderate spirit in which they accomplished it.

III

The Nonjuring schism was by no means the only difficulty which the Church of England had to confront in these troubled years. The definition of her relationship with State and nation, if at the moment it

aroused less bitterness, was in the long
run more intricate in its nature. That
some sort of toleration was inevitable few,
save a group of prejudiced irreconcilables,
would have denied. But greater things
were in the air, and there were still many
who dreamed of a grand scheme of Com-
prehension, by which all save the more
extreme Dissenters would have been admitted to the Church. It is this which
explains the acrimonious debates of the
next two years. The hatred of the Church
for dissent can only be understood by
those who study with care the insults
heaped upon her by the sectaries during
the Civil Wars. That men who had
striven for her dissolution should be admitted to her privileges seemed to Churchmen as tragic as ironical. Nor must we
miss the political aspect of the matter.
William had received an eager, if natural,
support from Nonconformists; and since
the vast majority of them was Whig in
temper, the greater the degree of toleration, the greater likelihood there was of
an attack upon the Church. Exclusion
thus became a fundamental article of the
Tory creed; and it was the more valued

because it enabled them to strike at their opponents through an institution which at the trial of Sacheverell, in 1710, still showed an overwhelming hold upon the mass of the people.

The attitude of mind herein implied is in large part the reaction from the Erastian temper of the government. Under William, that temper is intelligible enough; for unless he held the Church in strict control, he must have felt that he was giving a large handle to his enemies. Under Anne, the essence of the situation remained unchanged, even though her eager sympathy with the Church was beyond all question. William had relieved Nonconformists from the burden of penal statute; the Occasional Conformity Act of 1713 broadly continued the exclusion of all save the more yielding of them from political office. When the Hanoverians succeeded they were willing to repeal its more rigid intolerance; but the Test Act remained as evidence that the Dissenters were not yet regarded as in a full sense part of the national life.

The reasons for the hatred of dissent go back in part to the Civil War and in part also to the feeling of common ground between the dissenting interest and Rome which was born of the struggle under Elizabeth and James. The pamphlets are innumerable; and most of them deserve the complete obliquity into which they have fallen. We are told, in the eighteenth as in the seventeenth century, that the Presbyterian theory of government is inconsistent with the existence of the civil power. "They claim," said Leslie, "power to abrogate the laws of the land touching ecclesiastical matters, if they judge them hurtful or unprofitable. . . . They require the civil magistrate to be subject to their power." Of Knox or Cartwright this is no unfair account; but of the later Presbyterians it is the merest travesty. It supposes that they would be willing to push to the utmost limit the implications of the theory of the two kingdoms — a supposition which their passive submission to the Act of 1712 restoring lay patronage decisively refutes. Bramhall had no doubt that their discipline was "the very quintessence of refined popery," and the argument is repeated by a hundred less learned pamphleteers. Neither the grim irony of

Defoe nor the proven facts of the case could wean either the majority of Churchmen or the masses of the people from the belief that the Revolution endangered the very existence of the Church and that concession would be fatal. So stoutly did the Church resist it that the accession of George I alone, in Lecky's view, prevented the repeal of the Toleration Act and the destruction of the political benefits of the Revolution.

But nowhere was the temper of the time more clearly displayed than in the disputes over Convocation. To William's advisers, perhaps, more than to the Church itself their precipitation is due; for had they not, at the outset of the reign, suggested large changes in the liturgy suspicions then aroused might well have slumbered. As it was, the question of the royal supremacy immediately came into view and the clergy spared no effort to meet the issue so raised. And this they felt the more bitterly because the upper house of Convocation, two-thirds of which were William's nominees, naturally inclined to his side. Both under William and Anne the dispute continued, and the lower clergy shrank from no opportunity of conflict. They fought the king, the archbishop, the upper house. They attacked the writings of Toland and Burnet, the latter's book since recognized as one of the great treasures of Anglican literature. In the main, of course, the struggle was part of the perennial conflict between High Church doctrine and latitudinarianism. But that was only a fragment of the issue. What really was in question was the nature of the State's power over the Church. That could be left unanswered so long, as with James I and Charles, the two powers had but a single thought. The situation changed only when State and Church had different policies to fulfil and different means for their attainment.

The controversy had begun on the threshold of William's accession; but its real commencement dates from 1697. In that year was published the *Letter to a Convocation Man,* probably written by Sir Bartholomew Shower, an able if unscrupulous Jacobite lawyer, which maliciously, though with abounding skill, raised every question that peaceful

churchmen must have been anxious to
avoid. The *Letter* pointed out the growth
of infidelity and the increasing suspicion
that the Church was becoming tainted
with Socinian doctrine. Only the assembly of Convocation could arrest these
evils. The author did not deny that the
king's assent was necessary to its
summons. But he argued that once the
Convocation had met, it could, like Parliament, debate all questions relevant to its
purpose. "The one of these courts," said
Shower, "is of the same power and use
with regard to the Church as the other is
in respect to the State," and he insisted
that the writ of summons could not at any
point confine debate. And since the Convocation was an ecclesiastical Parliament,
it followed that it could legislate and thus
make any canons "provided they do not
impugn common law, statutes, customs or
prerogative." "To confer, debate and
resolve," said Shower, "without the king's
license, is at common law the undoubted
right of convocation."

Here was a clear challenge which was
at once answered, in *The Authority of
Christian Princes,* by William Wake, who

was by far the most learned of the latitudinarian clergy, and the successor of Tenison in the see of Canterbury. His argument was purely historical. He endeavored to show that the right to summon ecclesiastical synods was always the prerogative of the early Christian princes until the aggression of the popes had won church independence. The Reformation resumed the primitive practice; and the Act of Submission of 1532 had made it legally impossible for the clergy to discuss ecclesiastical matters without royal permission. Historically, the argument of Wake was irrefutable; but what mostly impressed the Church was the uncompromising Erastianism of his tone. Princes, he said, "may make what laws or constitutions they think fit for the Church. . . . a canon is but as matter prepared for the royal stamp." In this view, obviously, the Church is more than a department of the State. But Wake went even farther, "I cannot see why the Supreme Magistrate," he wrote, "who confessedly has a power to confirm or reject their (Convocation's) decrees, may not also make such other use of them as he pleases, and cor-

rect, improve, or otherwise alter their res-
olutions, according to his own liking,
before he gives his authority to them."

So defined no Church could claim in
any true sense the headship of Christ; for
it was clearly left at the mercy of the governmental view of expedient conduct.
Wake's answer aroused a sensation almost
as acute as the original *Letter* of Shower.
But by far the ablest criticism it provoked
was that of Francis Atterbury, then a
young student of Christ Church and on
the threshold of his turbulent career. His
*Rights, Powers and Privileges of an
English Convocation Stated and Vindi-
cated* not only showed a masterly historic
sense in its effort to traverse the unanswerable induction of Wake, but challenged his position more securely on the
ground of right. The historical argument, indeed, was not a safe position for
the Church, and Wake's rejoinder in his
State of the Church (1703) is generally
conceded to have proved his point, so far
as the claim of prescription is concerned.
But when Atterbury moves to the deeper
problem of what is involved in the nature
of a church, he has a powerful plea to

make. It is unnecessary now to deal with
his contention that Wake's defence of the
Royal Supremacy undermines the rights
of Parliament; for Wake could clearly
reply that the seat of that power had
changed with the advent of the Revolution. Where the avoidance of sympathy
is difficult is in his insistence that no
Church can live without an assembly to
debate its problems, and that no assembly
can be real which is subject to external
control. "Their body," as he remarks,
"will be useless to the State and by consequence contemptible"; for its opinions
will not be born of that free deliberation
which can alone ensure respect. Like all
High Churchmen, Atterbury has a clear
sense that Church and State can no longer
be equated, and he is anxious to preserve
the personality of the Church from the in-
vasions of an alien body. To be real, it
must be independent, and to be independent, it must have organs of self-expres-
sion. But neither William nor Anne
could afford to forego the political capital
involved in ecclesiastical control and Erastian principles proceeded to their triumph.

Here, as elsewhere, it was Charles

Leslie who best summed up the feeling of
High Churchmen. His *Case of the Regale* (1701) is by far the ablest of his
many able performances. He saw at the
outset that the real issue was defined by
the Church's claim to be a divine society,
with rights thus consecrated by the conditions of its origin. If it was divine, invasion did not touch its *de jure* rights.
"How," he asked, "can rights that are
divine be given up? If they are divine,
no human authority can either supersede
or limit them. . . . How can rights that
are inherent be given up? If they are
inherent, they are inseparable. The right
to meet, to consult, to make rules or
canons for the regulation of the society, is
essential to every society as such . . .
can she then part with what is essential to
her?" Nor could it be denied that "where
the choice of the governors of one society
is in the hands of another society, that
society must be dependent and subject to
the other." The Church, in the Latitudinarian view was thus either the creature of
the state or an *imperium in imperio;* but
Leslie would not admit that fruitful
stumbling block to the debate. "The

sacred and civil powers were like two
parallel lines which could never meet or
interfere . . . the confusion arises . . .
when the civil power will take upon them
to control or give laws to the Church, in
the exercise of her spiritual authority."
He did not doubt that the Church should
give securities for its loyalty to the king,
and renounce any effort at the coercion of
the civil magistrate. But the Church was
entitled to a similar privilege, and kings
should not "have their beneficence and
protection to the Church of Christ understood as a bribe to her, to betray and de-
liver up into their hands the powers com-
mitted into her charge by Christ."   Nor
did he fail to point out the suicidal nature
of Erastianism. For the church's hold
upon men is dependent upon their faith in
the   independence   of   her   principles.
"When they see bishops," he wrote wisely,
"made by the Court, they are apt to imagine that they speak to them the court
language; and lay no further stress upon
it than the charge of a judge at an assizes,
who has received his instructions before-
hand from the Court; and by this means
the state has lost the greatest security of
her government."

The argument is powerful enough; though it should be noted that some of its implications remain undetermined. Leslie does not say how the spheres of Church and State are to be differentiated. He does not explain the methods whereby an establishment is to be made compatible with freedom. For it is obvious that the partnership of Church and State must be upon conditions; and once the State had permitted the existence of creeds other than that of its official adoption, it could not maintain the exclusive power for which the Church contended. And when the Church not only complained of State-betrayal, but attempted the use of political means to enforce remedial measures it was inevitable that statesmen would use the weapons ready to their hand to coerce it to their will. The real remedy for the High Churchmen was not exclusiveness but disestablishment.

That this is the meaning of the struggle did not appear until the reign of George I. What is known as the Bangorian controversy was due to the posthumous publication, in 1716, of the papers of George Hickes, the most celebrated of the Non-

jurors in his generation. The papers are
of no special import; but taken in connection with the Jacobite rising of 1715
they seemed to imply a new attack upon
the Revolution settlement. So, at least,
they were interpreted by Benjamin
Hoadly, then Bishop of Bangor, and a
stout upholder of the Latitudinarian
school. The conflict today has turned to
dust and ashes; and few who read the
multitude of pamphlets it evoked, or stand
amazed at their personal bitterness, can
understand why more than a hundred
writers should have thought it necessary
to inform the world of their opinions, or
why the London Stock Exchange should
have felt so passionate an interest in the
debate as to cease for a day the hubbub
of its transactions. Nor can any one
make heroes from the personalities of its
protagonists. Hoadly himself was a
typical bishop of the political school, who
rose from humble circumstances to the
wealthy bishopric of Winchester through
a remarkable series of translations. Before the debate of 1716, he was chiefly
known by two political tracts in which he
had rewritten, in less cogent form, and

without adequate acknowledgment, the two treatises of Locke. He clearly realized how worthless the dogma of Divine Right had become, without being certain of the principles by which it was to be replaced. Probably, as Leslie Stephen has pointed out, his theorizing is the result of a cloudy sense of the bearing of the Deist controversy. If God is to be banished from direct connection with earthly affairs, we must seek a human explanation of political facts. And he became convinced that this attitude applies not less completely to ecclesiastical than to secular politics. Of his opponents, by far the ablest was William Law, the only theologian whom Gibbon may be said to have respected, and the parent, through his mystical writings, of the Wesleyan movement. Snape, then Provost of Eton, was always incisive; and his pamphlet went through seventeen editions in a single year and provoked seven replies within three months. Thomas Sherlock would not be either himself or his father's son, were he not caustic, logical and direct. But Hoadly and Law between them exhaust the controversy, so far as it has meaning for our own day. The less essential questions like Hoadly's choice of friends, his attitude to prayer, the accuracy of the details in his account of the Test Act, the cause of his refusal to answer Law directly, are hardly now germane to the substance of the debate. Hoadly's position is most fully stated in his *Preservative against the Principles and Practice of Nonjurors* which he published in 1716 as a counterblast to the papers of Hickes; and they are briefly summarized in the sermon preached before the King on March 31, 1717, on the text "My Kingdom is not of this world," and published by royal command. Amid a vast wilderness of quibbles and qualifications, some simple points emerge. What he was doing was to deprive the priesthood of claims to supernatural authority that he might vindicate for civil government the right to preserve itself not less against persons in ecclesiastical office than against civil assailants. To do so he is forced to deny that the miraculous powers of Christ and the Apostles descended to their successors. For if that assumption is made we grant to fallible

men privileges which confessedly belong
to persons outside the category of falli-
bility. And, exactly in the fashion of
Leslie in the *Regale* he goes on to show
that if a Church is a supernatural institution, it cannot surrender one jot or tittle of
its prerogative. It is, in fact, an *imperium
in imperio* and its conflict with the state is
inevitable. But if the Church is not a supernatural institution, what is its nature?
Hoadly here attacks the doctrine which
lies at the basis of all ecclesiastical debate.
The Church, he claims, is not a visible society, presided over by men who have authority directly transmitted by Christ.
There are not within it "viceregents who
can be said properly to supply his place;
no interpreters upon whom his subjects
are absolutely to depend; no judges over
the conscience or religion of his people.
For if this were so that any such absolute
viceregent authority, either for the making of new laws, or interpreting old ones,
or judging his subjects, in religious
matters, were lodged in any men upon
earth, the consequence would be that what
still retains the name of the Church of
Christ would not be the kingdom of

Christ, but the kingdom of those men invested with such authority. For whoever hath such an authority of making laws is so far a king, and whoever can add new laws to those of Christ, equally obligatory, is as truly a king as Christ himself. Nay, whosoever hath an absolute authority to interpret any written or spoken laws, it is he who is truly the lawgiver to all intents and purposes, and not the person who first wrote and spoke them."

The meaning is clear enough. What Hoadly is attacking is the theory of a visible Church of Christ on earth, with the immense superstructure of miracle and infallibility erected thereon. The true Church of Christ is in heaven; and the members of the earthly society can but try in a human, blundering way, to act with decency and justice. Apostolic succession, the power of excommunication, the dealing out of forgiveness for men's sins, the determination of true doctrine, insofar as the Church claims these powers, it is usurping an authority that is not its own. The relation of man to God is his private affair, and God will ask from him sincerity and honesty, rather than judge

him for his possession of some special set
of dogmas. Clearly, therefore, if the
Church is no more than this, it has no supernatural pretensions to oppose to the
human claims of the State. And since the
State must have within itself all the means
of sufficient life, it has the right to resist
the ecclesiastical onslaught as based upon
the usurpation of power assumed without
right. And in later treatises Hoadly did
for ceremonial exactly what he had done
for church government. The eucharist
became a piece of symbolism and excommunication nothing more than an an-
nouncement — "a mere external thing"
— that the rules of the fellowship have
been broken. It at no point is related to
the sinner's opportunity of salvation.

In such an aspect, it would clearly follow that the Church has no monopoly of
truth. It can, indeed, judge its own beliefs; but reason alone can demonstrate
the inadequacy of other attitudes. Nor
does its judgment preclude the individual
duty to examine into the truth of things.
The real root of faith is not the possession
of an infallible dogma, but the arriving
honestly at the dogma in which you

happen to believe. For the magistrate,
he urges, what is important is not the table
of your springs of action, but the conduct
itself which is based upon that table; from
which it follows that things like the Test
and Corporation Acts have no real political validity. They have been imposed
upon the State by the narrow interpre-
tations of an usurping power; and the
Nonconformist claim to citizenship would
thus seem as valid as that of a member of
the Church of England.

All this sounds sensible enough; though
it is curious doctrine in the mouth of a
bishop of that church. And this, in fact,
is the starting-point of Law's analysis of
Hoadly. No one who reads the unsparing
vigor of his criticism can doubt that Law
must have been thoroughly happy in the
composition of his defence; and, indeed,
his is the only contribution to the debate
which may claim a permanent place in political literature. In one sense, indeed, the
whole of Law's answer is an *ignoratio
elenchi,* for he assumes the truth of that
which Hoadly sets out to examine, with
the inevitable result that each writer is, for
the most part, arguing from different

premises. But on the assumption that
Hoadly is a Christian, Law's argument
is an attack of great power. He shows
conclusively that if the Church of England is no more than Hoadly imagines it
to be, it cannot, in any proper historic
sense, be called the Church of England
at all. For every one of the institutions
which Hoadly calls an usurpation, is believed by Churchmen to be integral to its
nature. And if sincerity alone is to count
as the test, then there cannot, for the existing world, be any such thing as objective religious truth. It subverted not
merely absolute authority — which the
Church of England did not claim — but
any authority in the Church. It impugned
the authority of the Crown to enforce religious belief by civil penalties. Hoadly's
rejection of authority, moreover, is in
Law's view fatal to government of any
kind. For all lawful authority must affect
eternal salvation insofar as to disobey it
is to sin. The authority the Church possesses is inherent in the very nature of the
Church; for the obligation to a belief in
Christianity is the same thing as to a belief in that Church which can be shown to
represent Christ's teaching.

From Law's own point of view, the
logic of his position is undeniable; and in
his third letter to Hoadly, the real heart
of his attack, he touches the centre of the
latter's argument. For if it is sincerity
which is alone important it would follow
that things false and wrong are as acceptable to God as things true and right, which
is patently absurd. Nor has Hoadly
given us means for the detection of sincerity. He seemed to think that anyone
was sincere who so thought himself; but,
says Law, "it is also possible and as likely
for a man to be mistaken in those things
which constitute true sincerity as in those
things which constitute true religion."
Clearly, sincerity cannot be the pith of
the matter; for it may be mistaken and
directed to wrong ends. The State, in
fact, may respect conscience, but Hoadly
is no more entitled to assume the infallibility of private belief than he is to deny
the infallibility of the Church's teaching.
That way lies anarchy.

Here, indeed, the antagonists were on
common ground. Both had denied the
absolute character of any authority; but
while Hoadly virtually postulates a

Church which logically is no more than
those who accept the moral law as Christ
described it, Law restricts the Church to
that society which bears the traditional
marks of the historic institution. On
Hoadly's principles, there was no reason
why anyone not hostile to the civil power
should not enjoy political privilege; on
Law's there was every reason simply because those who denied the doctrines of
the High Church refused a truth open
for their acceptance. Law, indeed, goes
so far as to argue that in the light of his
principles Hoadly should be a Deist; and
there is ground for what, in that age, was
a valuable point to make. The sum total
of it all is that for the bishop the outward
actions of men alone concern the State;
while Law insists that the root of action
and the test of fitness is whether men have
seen a certain aspect of the truth and
grasped it.

The result, to say the least, was calami-
tous. In May of 1717, convocation met
and the Lower House immediately
adopted an unanimous report condemning
the "Preservative" and the sermon. But
Hoadly had the government behind him

and the convocation was prorogued before
further action could be taken. Snape,
Hare, Mosse and Sherlock, all of whom
were chaplains royal, and had been drawn
into the conflict, were dismissed from
their office; and for more than one hundred and thirty-five years convocation was
not again summoned. It was a striking
triumph for Erastianism, though the more
liberal principles of Hoadly were less successful. Robert Walpole was on the
threshold of his power, and, as a manager
of Sacheverell's impeachment, he had seen
the hold of the Church upon the common
people, may even, indeed, have remembered that Hoadly's own dwelling had
been threatened with destruction in the
popular excitement. *Quieta non movere*
was his motto; and he was not interested
in the niceties of ecclesiastic metaphysic.
So the Test Act remained immovable until
1828; while the annual Act of Indemnity
for its infractions represented that English genius for illogical mitigation which
solves the deeper problems of principle
while avoiding the consideration of their
substance.

In the hundred and twenty years which

passed between the Bangorian Controversy and the Oxford Movement, there is
only one volume upon the problem of
Church and State which deserves more
than passing notice. Bishop Warburton
was the Lord Brougham of his age; and
as its self-constituted universal provider
of intellectual fare, he deemed it his duty
to settle this, amongst others of the
eternal questions. The effort excited only
the contempt of Leslie Stephen — "the
peculiar Warburton mixture," he says "of
sham logic and bluster." Yet that is
hardly fair to the total result of Warburton's remarks. He tried to steer a
middle path between the logical result of
such Erastianism as that of the *Independent Whig,* on the one hand, and the ex-
cessive claim of High Churchmanship on
the other. Naturally enough, or the
writer would not be Warburton, the book
is full of tawdry rhetoric and stupid
quibbles. But the *Alliance between
Church and State* (1736) set the temper
of speculation until the advent of Newman, and is therefore material for something more than contempt. It acutely
points out that societies generate a per-

sonality distinct from that of their members in words reminiscent of an historic legal pronouncement.[1] "When any number of men," he says, "form themselves into a society, whether civil or religious, this society becomes a body different from that aggregate which the number of individuals composed before the society was formed. . . . But a body must have its proper personality and will, which without these is no more than a shadow or a name."

And that is the root of Warburton's pronouncement. The Church is a society distinct from the State, but lending to that body its assistance because without the sanction of religion the full achievement of the social purpose is impossible. There is thus an alliance between them, each lending its support to the other for their common benefit. The two remain distinct; the union between them is of a federal kind. But they interchange their powers, and this it is which explains at once the royal supremacy and the right of Churchmen to a share in the legislature.

[1] Dicey, *Law and Opinion in England* (2nd edition), p. 165.

This also it is which explains the existence of a Test Act, whereby those who might injure that which the State has undertaken to protect are deprived of their power to evil. And, in return, the Church engages to "apply its utmost endeavors in the service of the State." It becomes attached to its benefactor from the privilege it receives; and the dangers which might arise from its natural independence are thus obviated. For a federal union precludes the grave problem of an *imperium in imperio,* and the "mischiefs which so terrified Hobbes" are met by the terms upon which it is founded.

It is easy enough to discover the loopholes in the theory. The contract does not exist, or, at least, it is placed by Warburton "in the same archive with the famous original compact between monarch and people" which has been the object of vast but fruitless searches. Nor does the Act of Submission bear upon its face the marks of that tender care of the protection of an independent society which Warburton declared a vital tenet of the Union. Yet such criticisms miss the real significance of the theory. It is really the in-

troduction into English politics of that
notion of the two societies which, a century before, Melville and Bellarmine had
made so fruitful. With neither Presbyterian nor Jesuit was the separation complete, for the simple reason that each had
a secret conviction that the ecclesiastical
society was at bottom the superior. Yet
the theory was the parent of liberty, if
only because it pointed the way to a balance of power between claims which, before, had seemed mutually exclusive.

Until the Toleration Act, the theory
was worthless to the English Church because its temper, under the ægis of
Laudian views, had been in substance
theocratic. But after 1692 it aptly expressed the compromise the dominant
party of the Church had then in mind.
They did, indeed, mistake the power of
the Church, or, rather, they submitted to
the State so fully that what they had intended for a partnership became an absorption. So that the Erastianism of the
eighteenth century goes deep enough to
make the Church no more than a moral
police department of the State. Saints
like Ken and preachers like South are re-

placed by fashionable prelates like Cornwallis, who made Lambeth Palace an adjunct to Ranelagh Gardens, and self-seek-
ing pluralists like Bishop Watson. The
Church could not even perceive the meaning of the Wesleyan revolt; and its charity
was the irritating and complacent patronage of the obstrusive Hannah More. Its
learning decayed, its intelligence slumbered; and the main function it fulfilled
until Newman's advent was the provision
of rich preferment to the younger sons of
the nobility. It is a far cry from Lake
of Chichester and Bishop Ken to a church
which was merely an annex to the iniquities of the civil list.

IV

No one can mistake the significance of
this conflict. The opponents of Erastianism had a deep sense of their corporate
Church, and it was a plea for ecclesiastical
freedom that they were making. They
saw that a Church whose patronage and
discipline and debates were under the
control of an alien body could not with
honesty claim that Christ was in truth

their head. If the Church was to be at
the mercy of private judgment and political expediency, the notion of a dogmatic
basis would have to be abandoned. Here,
indeed, is the root of the condemnation of
Tindal and of Hoadly; for they made it,
by their teaching, impossible for the
Church to possess an ethos of her own. It
was thus against the sovereignty of the
State that they protested. Somewhere, a
line must be drawn about its functions that
the independence of the Church might be
safeguarded. For its supporters could
not be true to their divine mission if the
accidental vote of a secular authority was
by right to impose its will upon the
Church. The view of it as simply a religious body to which the State had conceded certain rights and dignities, they
repudiated with passion. The life of the
Church was not derived from the State;
and for the latter to attempt its circum-
scription was to usurp an authority not
rightly its own.

The real difficulty of this attitude lay in
the establishment. For here the Church
was, at bottom, declaring that the State
life must be lived upon terms of her own

definition. That was possible before the Reformation; but with the advent of Nonconformity and the growth of rationalism the exclusive character of the Church's solution had become unacceptable. If the Church was to become so intimately involved with the State as an establishment implied, it had no right to complain, if statesmen with a genius for expediency were willing to sacrifice it to the attainment of that ideal. For the real secret of independence is, after all, no more than independence. The Church sought it without being willing to pay the price. And this it is which enabled Hoadly to emerge triumphant from an ordeal where logically he should have failed. The State, by definition is an absorptive animal; and the Church had no right to complain if the price of its privileges was royal supremacy. A century so self-satisfied as the eighteenth would not have faced the difficulties involved in giving political expression to the High Church theory.

Yet the protest remained, and it bore a noble fruit in the next century. The Oxford movement is usually regarded as a return to the seventeenth century, to

the ideals, that is to say, of Laud and
Andrewes.[1] In fact, its real kinship is
with Atterbury and Law. Like them, it
was searching the secret of ecclesiastical
independence, and like them it discovered
that connection with the State means, in
the end, the sacrifice of the church to the
needs of each political situation. "The
State has deserted us," wrote Newman;
and the words might have been written of
the earlier time. The Oxford movement,
indeed, like its predecessor, built upon
foundations of sand; and when Lord
Brougham told the House of Lords that
the idea of the Church possessing "absolute and unalienable rights" was a "gross
and monstrous anomaly" because it would
make impossible the supremacy of Parliament, he simply announced the result of
a doctrine which, implicit in the Act of
Submission, was first completely defined
by Wake and Hoadly. Nor has the
history of this controversy ended.
"Thoughtful men," the Archbishop of
Canterbury has told the House of Lords, [2]

[1] Cf. my *Problem of Sovereignty*, Chapter III.
[2] *Parliamentary Debates*. Fifth Series, Vol. 34,
p. 992 (June 3, 1919).

". . . see the absolute need, if a Church is to be strong and vigorous, for the Church, *qua* church, to be able to say what it can do as a church." "The rule of the sovereign, the rule of Parliament," replied Lord Haldane,[1] "extend as far as the rule of the Church. They are not to be distinguished or differentiated, and that was the condition under which ecclesiastical power was transmitted to the Church of England." Today, that is to say, as in the past, antithetic theories of the nature of the State hinge, in essence, upon the problem of its sovereignty. "A free church in a free state," now, as then, may be our ideal; but we still seek the means wherewith to build it.

[1] *Parliamentary Debates.* Fifth Series, Vol. 34, p. 1002. The quotation does not fully represent Lord Haldane's views.

CHAPTER IV

THE ERA OF STAGNATION

I

WITH the accession of George I, there ensued an era of unexampled calm in English politics, which lasted until the expulsion of Walpole from power in 1742. No vital questions were debated, nor did problems of principle force themselves into view; and if the Jacobites remained in the background as an element invincibly hostile to absorption, the failure of their effort in 1715 showed how feeble was their hold on English opinion. Not, indeed, that the new dynasty was popular. It had nothing of that romantic glamour of a lost cause so imperishably recorded in Scott's pages. The first Georges were heavy and foreign and meagre-souled; but at least they were Protestant, and, until the reign of George III, they were amenable to management. In the result, an opposition in the classic sense was hardly needed; for the only question to be considered was the personalities who were to share in power. The dominating temper of Walpole decided that issue; and he gave thereby to the political struggle the outlines in which it was encased for a generation.

It is a dull period, but complacent; for it was not an unprosperous time. Agriculture and commerce both were abundant; and the increasing development of towns shows us that the Industrial Revolution loomed in the near distance. The eager continuance of the deistic controversy suggests that there was something of novelty beneath the calm; for Tindal and Woolston and Chubb struck at the root of religious belief, and Shaftesbury's exaltation of Hellenism not only contributed to the *Aufklarung* in Scotland, but suggested that Christian ideals were not to go unchallenged. But the literature of the time is summarized in Pope; and the easy neatness of his verses is quaintly representative of the Georgian peace. Defoe and Swift had both done their work; and the latter had withdrawn to Ireland to

die like a rat in a hole. Bishop Berkeley,
indeed, was convinced of the decadence of
England; but his *Essay towards Preventing the Ruin of Great Britain* (1721)
shows rather the effect of the speculative
mania which culminated in the South Sea
Bubble upon a noble moral nature than
a genius for political thought. Certainly
no one in that generation was likely to
regard with seriousness proposals for the
endowment of motherhood and a tax upon
the estate of bachelors. The cynical soph-
istries of Mandeville were, despite the indignation they aroused, more suited to
the age that Walpole governed. It is, in
fact, the character of the minister which
sets the keynote of the time. An able
speaker, without being a great orator, a
superb administrator, eager rather for
power than for good, rating men low by
instinct and corrupting them by intelligence, Walpole was not the man, either in
type of mind or of temperament, to bring
great questions to the foreground of debate. He was content to maintain his
hold over the respect of the Crown, and
to punish able rivals by exclusion from
office. One by one, the younger men of

talent, Carteret, Pulteney, Chesterfield, Pitt, were driven into hostility. He maintained himself in office by a corruption as efficiently administered as it was cynically conceived. An opposition developed less on principle than on the belief that spoils are matter rather for distribution than for concentration. The party so formed had, indeed, little ground save personal animosity upon which to fight; and its ablest exertions could only seize upon a doubtful insult to a braggart sea-captain as the pretext of the war it was Walpole's ambition no less than policy to avoid. From 1726 until 1735 the guiding spirit of the party was Bolingbroke; but in the latter year he quarrelled with Pulteney, nominally its leader, and retired in high dudgeon to France. But in the years of his leadership he had evolved a theory of politics than which nothing so clearly displays the intellectual bankruptcy of the time.

To understand the argument of Bolingbroke it is necessary to remember the peculiar character of his career. He had attained to the highest office under Anne at an exceptionally early age; and his

period of power had been distinguished by
the vehemence with which he pursued the
ideal of a strict division of parties and the
expulsion of all alien elements from the
government. But he had staked all his
fortunes upon a scheme he had neither the
resolution to plan nor the courage to exe-
cute; and his flight to France, on the Han-
overian accession, had been followed by
his proscription. Walpole soon succeeded
alike to his reputation and place; and
through an enormous bribe to the bottom-
less pocket of the King's mistress St.
John was enabled to return from exile,
though not to political place. His restless
mind was dissatisfied with exclusion from
power, and he occupied himself with creating an alliance between the Tories and
malcontent Whigs for Walpole's overthrow. The alliance succeeded, though
too late for Bolingbroke to enjoy the
fruits of success; but in effecting the purgation of the Tory party from its taint of
Jacobitism he rendered no inconsiderable
service. His foundation, moreover, of the
Craftsman — the first official journal of
a political party in England — showed his
appreciation of the technique of political

controversy. Most of it is dead now, and, indeed, no small part of its contemporary success is due to the making of comment in terms of the immediate situation, as also by its consistent use of a personal reference which has, save in the mass, no meaning for today. Though, doubtless, the idea of its inception was derived from journals like Defoe's *Review* and Leslie's *Rehearsal,* which had won success, its intimate connection with the party leadership was a novel element; and it may therein claim a special relation to the official periodicals of a later generation.

The reputation of Bolingbroke as a political philosopher is something that our age can hardly understand. "A solemn trifler," Lord Morley has called him; and it is difficult to know why his easy declamation was so long mistaken for profound thought. Much, doubtless, is due to that personal fascination which made him the inspiration of men so different as Pope and Voltaire; and the man who could supply ideas to Chatham and Disraeli cannot be wholly devoid of merit. Certainly he wrote well, in that easy elegance of style which was the delight of the eighteenth century; and he is consistently happy in his choice of adjectives. But his work is at every point embellished with that affectation of classical learning which was the curse of his age. He sought no general truths, and he is free from the accusation of sincerity. Nor has he any enthusiasm save that of bitter partisanship. He hated Walpole, and his political writings are, at bottom, no more than an attempt to generalize his animosity. The *Dissertation on Parties* (1734) and the *Idea of a Patriot King* (1738) might have betrayed us, taken alone, into regarding their author as a disinterested observer watching with regret the development of a fatal system; but taken in conjunction with the *Letter to Sir W. Windham* (1717), which was not published until after his death, and is written with an acrid cynicism fatal to his claim to honesty, they reveal the opinions as no more than a mask for ambition born of hate.

The whole, of course, must have some sort of background; and the *Letters on the Study of History* (1735) was doubtless intended to supply it. Experience is to be the test of truth, since history is phil-

osophy teaching by example. But Bolingbroke's own argument supplies its refutation. His history is an arbitrary selection
of instances intended to illustrate the particular ideas which happened to be uppermost in his mind. The Roman consuls
were chosen by annual election; whence it
is clear that England should have, if not
an annual, at least a triennial parliament.
He acknowledges that the past in some
degree unknown determines the present.
He has some not unhappy remarks upon
the evils of an attitude which fails to look
upon events from a larger aspect than
their immediate environment. But his
history is intended less to illustrate the
working of principle than to collect cases
worthy of citation. Time and space do
not exist as categories; he is as content
with a Roman anecdote as with a Stuart
illustration. He is willing, indeed, to
look for the causes of the Revolution as
far back as the reign of James I; though
he shows his lack of true perception when
he ascribes the true inwardness of the
Reformation to the greed of the monarch
for the spoils of the clergy. At bottom
what mainly impresses him is the immense

influence of personal accident upon events. Intrigue, a sudden dislike, some backstairs piece of gossip, here is the real root of great changes. And when he expresses a "thorough contempt" for the kind of work scholars such as Scaliger and Petavius had achieved, he shows his entire ignorance of the method whereby alone a knowledge of general principle can be attained.

A clear vision, of course, he has, and he was not beguiled by high notions of prerogative or the like. The divine right of kings is too stupid to be worth the trouble of refutation; all that makes a king important is the authority he exerts. So, too, with the Church; for Bolingbroke, as a professed deist, has no trouble with such matters as the apostolic succession. He makes great show of his love of liberty, which is the true end of government; and we are informed with a vast solemnity of the "perpetual danger" in which it always stands. So that the chief end of patriotism is its maintenance; though we are never told what liberty is, nor how it is to be maintained. The social compact seems to win his approbation and we learn that the

secret of the British constitution is the
balance of powers and their mutual inde-
pendency. But what the powers are, and
how their independence is preserved we do
not learn, save by an insistence that the
safety of Europe is to be found in playing
off the ambitions of France and Austria
against each other; an analogy the rejection of which has been the secret of English constitutional success. We learn of
the evil of standing armies and the danger
of Septennial Parliaments. We are told
that parties are mainly moved by the prospect of enjoying office and vast patronage; and a great enough show is made of
his hatred for corruption as to convince at
least some critics of distinction of his sincerity. The parties of the time had, as he
sees, become divided by no difference save
that of interest; and herein, at least, he
shows us how completely the principles of
the Revolution had become exhausted.
He wants severe penalties upon electoral
corruption. He would have disfranchised
the rotten boroughs and excluded place-
men from Parliament. The press was to
be free; and there is at least a degree of
generous insight in his plea for a wider

commercial freedom in colonial matters.
Yet what, after all, does this mean save
that he is fighting a man with the patronage at his disposal and a majority upon
the committee for the settlement of disputed elections? And what else can we
see in his desire for liberty of the press
save a desire to fight Walpole in the open,
without fear of the penalties his former
treason had incurred?

His value can be tested in another way.
His *Idea of a Patriot King* is the remedy
for the ills he has depicted. He was sixty
years old when it appeared, and he had
then been in active politics for thirty-five
years, so that we are entitled to regard it
as the fruit of his mature experience. He
was too convinced that the constitution
was "in the strictest sense a bargain, a
conditional contract between the prince
and the people" to attempt again the erec-
tion of a system of prerogative. Yet it is
about the person of the monarch that the
theory hinges. He is to have no powers
inconsistent with the liberties of the
people; for such restraints will not shackle
his virtues while they limit the evil propen-
sities of a bad king. What is needed is a

patriot king who will destroy corruption
and awaken the spirit of liberty.   His
effective government will synchronize with
the commencement of his reign; and he
will at once dismiss the old and cunning
ministers, to replace them by servants who
are wise.   He will not stand upon party,
but upon the State.   He will unite the
forces of good counsel into a single
scheme.   Complaints will be answered, the
evildoers punished.   Commerce will flow
on with uninterrupted prosperity, and the
navy of England receive its due meed of
attention.   His conduct must be dignified,
and he must acquire his influence not
apart from, but on account of, the affection of his people.   "Concord," says Bolingbroke in rhapsodical prospection, "will
appear breeding peace and prosperity on
every hand"; though he prudently hopes
also that men will look back with affection
upon one "who desired life for nothing so
much as to see a King of Great Britain
the most powerful man in the country,
and a patriot King at the head of a united
people."

Bolingbroke himself has admitted that
such a monarch would be a "sort of stand-

ing miracle," and perhaps no other comment upon his system is required. A
smile in Plato at the sight of his phi-
losopher-King in such strange company
might well be pardoned. It is only necessary to point out that the person whom
Bolingbroke designates for this high function was Frederick, Prince of Wales, to
us the most meagre of a meagre generation, but to Bolingbroke, by whose grace
he was captivated, "the greatest and most
glorious of human beings." This exaltation of the monarch came at a time when
a variety of circumstances had combined
to show the decrease of monarchical sentiment. It bears upon its every page the
marks of a personal antagonism. It is too
obviously the programme of a party to be
capable of serious interpretation as a system. The minister who is to be impeached,
the wise servants who are to gain office,
the attack on corruption, the spirited
foreign policy — all these have the ear-
marks of a platform rather than of a philosophy. Attacks on corruption hardly
read well in the mouth of a dissolute
gambler; and the one solid evidence of
deep feeling is the remark on the danger

of finance in politics. For none of the
Tories save Barnard, who owed his party
influence thereto, understood the financial
schemes of Walpole; and since they were
his schemes obviously they represented the
triumph of devilish ingenuity. The return
of landed men to power would mean the
return of simplicity to politics; and one
can imagine the country squires, the last
resort of enthusiasm for Church and King,
feeling that Bolingbroke had here emphasized the dangers of a régime which already faintly foreshadowed their exclusion
from power. The pamphlet was the
cornerstone in the education of Frederick's son; and when George III came
to the throne he proceeded to give such
heed to his master as the circumstances
permitted. It is perhaps, as Mr. A. L.
Smith has argued, unfair to visit Bolingbroke with George's version of his ideal;
yet they are sufficiently connected for the
one to give the meaning to the other.
Chatham, indeed, was later intrigued by
this ideal of a national party; and before
Disraeli discovered that England does not
love coalitions he expended much rhetoric
upon the beauties of a patriotic king.

But Chatham was a wayward genius who had nothing of that instinct for common counsel which is of the essence of party government; while it is necessary to draw a firm line between Disraeli's genial declamation and his practice when in office. It is sufficient to say that the one effort founded upon the principles of Bolingbroke ended in disaster; and that his own last reflections express a bitter disillusion at the result of the event which he looked to as the inauguration of the golden age.

II

The fall of Walpole, indeed, released no energies for political thought; the system continued, though the men were different. What alone can be detected is the growth of a democratic opinion which found its sustenance outside the House of Commons, the opinion the strength of which was later to force the elder Pitt upon an unwilling king. An able pamphlet of the time shows us the arrival of this unlooked-for portent. *Faction detected by the Evidence of Facts* (1742)

was, though it is anonymous,[1] obviously
written by one in touch with the inner
current of affairs. The author had hoped
for the fall of Walpole, though he sees the
chaos in its result. "A republican spirit,"
he says, "has strangely arisen"; and he
goes on to tell how the electors of London
and Westminster were now regarding
their members as delegates to whom instructions might be issued. "A new party
of malcontents" had arisen, "assuming to
themselves, though very falsely, the title
of the People." They affect, he tells us,
"superiority to the whole legislature . . .
and endeavor in effect to animate the
people to resume into their own hands that
vague and loose authority which exists
(unless in theory) in the people of no
country upon earth, and the inconvenience
of which is so obvious that it is the first
step of mankind, when formed into society, to divest themselves of it, and to
delegate it forever from themselves." The
writer clearly foreshadows, even in his dislike, that temper which produced the
Wilkes affair, and made it possible for
Cartwright and Horne Tooke and Sir

[1] It was probably written by Lord Egmont.

Thomas Hollis to become the founders of English radicalism.

Yet the influence of that temper still lay a generation ahead; and the next piece of import comes from a mind which, though perhaps the most powerful of all which have applied themselves to political philosophy in England, was, from its very scepticism, incapable of constructive effort. David Hume was thirty-one years of age when he published (1742) the first series of his essays; and his *Treatise of Human Nature* which had fallen "dead-born from the press" was in some sort compensated by the success of the new work. The second part, entitled *Political Discourses,* was published in 1752, almost simultaneously with the *"Inquiry concerning the Principles of Morals."* As in the case of Hume's metaphysical studies, they constitute the most powerful dissolvent the century was to see. Yet nowhere was so clearly to be demonstrated the euthanasia into which English politics had fallen.

Hume, of course, is always critical and suggestive, and even if he had no distinctive contribution to make, he gave a new turn to speculation. There is something almost of magic in the ease with which he demolishes divine right and the social contract. The one is an inevitable deduction from theism, but it protects an usurper not less than an hereditary king, and gives a "divine commission" as well to a constable as to the most majestic prince. The proponents of the social contract are in no better case. "Were you to preach," he remarks, "in most parts of the world that political connections are founded altogether on voluntary consent, or on a mutual promise, the magistrate would soon imprison you as seditious for loosening the ties of obedience; if your friends did not before shut you up as delirious for advancing such absurdities." The original contract could not be produced, and, even if it were, it would suppose the "consent of the fathers to bind the children even to the most remote generations." The real truth, as he remarks, is that "almost all the governments which exist at present, or of which there remains any record in story, have been founded originally on usurpation, or on conquest, or both, without any pretence of a fair con-

sent or voluntary subjection of the
people." If we then ask why obedience is
possible, the sufficient answer is that "it
becomes so familiar that most men never
make any inquiry about its origin or cause,
any more than about the principle of
gravity, resistance, or the most universal
laws of nature."

Government, in short, is dependent
upon the inescapable facts of psychology.
It might be unnecessary if all desires could
be individually fulfilled by making them,
or if man showed to his fellow-men the
same tender regard he has for himself.
So happy a condition does not exist; and
government is the most useful way of
remedying the defects of our situation. A
theologian might say that Hume derives
government from original sin; to which he
would have replied by denying the fall.
His whole attitude is simply an insistence
that utility is the touchstone of institutions, and he may claim to be the first
thinker who attempted its application to
the whole field of political science. He
knows that opinion is the sovereign ruler
of mankind, and that ideas of utility lie
at the base of the thoughts which get ac-

cepted. He does not, indeed, deny that
fear and consent enter into the attitude of
men; he simply asserts that these also are
founded upon a judgment of utility in
the thing judged. We obey because
otherwise "society could not subsist," and
society subsists for its utility. "Men," he
says "could not live at all in society, at
least in a civilized society, without laws
and magistrates and judges, to prevent
the encroachments of the strong upon the
weak, of the violent upon the just and
equitable."

Utilitarianism is, of course, above all a
method; and it is not unfair to say of
Hume that he did not get very far beyond
insistence on that point. He sees that
the subjection of the many to the few is
rooted in human impulse; but he has no
penetrating inquiry, such as that of Locke
or Hobbes, into the purpose of such subjection. So, too, it is the sense of public
interest which determines men's thoughts
on government, on who should rule, and
what should be the system of property;
but the ethical substance of these questions
he leaves undetermined. Politics, he
thinks, may one day be a science; though

he considers the world still too young for general truths therein. The maxims he suggests as of permanent value, "that a hereditary prince, a nobility without vassals, and a people voting by their representatives form the best monarchy, autocracy and democracy"; that "free governments . . . are the most ruinous and oppressive to their provinces"; that republics are more favorable to science, monarchies to art; that the death of a political body is inevitable; would none of them, probably, be accepted by most thinkers at the present time. And when he constructs an ideal constitution, irrespective of time and place, which is to be regarded as practical because it resembles that of Holland, it is obvious that the historical method had not yet come fully into being.

Yet Hume is full of flashes of deep wisdom, and it would be an avoidance of justice not to note the extent of the spasmodic insight that he had. He has a keen eye for the absurdity of Pope's maxim that administration is all in all; nothing can ever make the forms of government immaterial. He accepts Harrington's

dictum that the substance of government
corresponds to the distribution of property, without making it, as later thinkers
have done, the foundation of all political
forces. He sees that the Crown cannot
influence the mass of men, or withstand
the new balance of property in the State;
a prophecy of which the accuracy was
demonstrated by the failure of George
III. "In all governments," as he says,
"there is a perpetual intestinal struggle,
open or secret," between Authority and
Liberty; though his judgment that
neither "can ever absolutely prevail,"
shows us rather that we are on the
threshold of *laissez-faire* than that Hume
really understood the problem of freedom.
He realized that the House of Commons
had become the pivot of the State; though
he looked with dread upon the onset of
popular government. He saw the inev-
itability of parties, as also their tendency
to persist in terms of men instead of principles. He was convinced of the necessity
of liberty to the progress of the arts and
sciences; and no one, save Adam Smith,
has more acutely insisted upon the evil
effect on commerce of an absolute govern-

ment. He emphasized the value of freedom of the press, in which he saw the
secret whereby the mixed government of
England was maintained. "It has also
been found," he said in a happy phrase,
". . . that the people are no such dangerous monsters as they have been represented, and that it is in every respect
better to guide them like rational creatures than to lead or drive them like brute
beasts." There is, in fact, hardly a page
of his work in which some such acuteness
may not be found.

Not, indeed, that a curious blindness is
absent. Hume was a typical child of one
aspect of the eighteenth century in his
hatred of enthusiasm, and the form in
which he most abominates it is religious.
Why people's religious opinions should
lead to antagonism he could no more understand than why people should refuse
to pass one another on a road. Wars of
religion thus seemed to him based upon a
merely frivolous principle; and in his ideal
commonwealth he made the Church a department of the State lest it should get out
of hand. He was, moreover, a static philosopher, disturbed by signs of political

restlessness; and this led to the purgation
of Whig doctrines from his writings, and
their consistent replacement by a cynical
conservatism. He was always afraid that
popular government would mean mob-
rule; and absolute government is accord-
ingly recommended as the euthanasia of
the British constitution. Not even the example of Sweden convinced him that a
standing army might exist without civil
liberty being endangered; and he has all
the noxious fallacies of his time upon the
balance of power. Above all, it is striking to see his helplessness before the problem of national character. Mainly he
ascribes it to the form of government, and
that in turn to chance. Even the friend of
Montesquieu can see no significance in
race or climate. The idea, in fact, of evolution is entirely absent from his political
speculation. Political life, like human
life, ends in death; and the problem is to
make our egress as comfortable as we can,
for the prime evil is disturbance. It is
difficult not to feel that there is almost a
physical basis in his own disease for this
love of quiet. The man who put indolence
among the primary motives of human

happiness was not likely to view novel theories with unruffled temper.

Hume has an eminent place among economists, and for one to whom the study of such phenomena was but a casual inquiry, it is marvelous how much he saw. He is free from the crude errors of mercantilism; and twenty years before Adam Smith hopes, "as a British subject," for the prosperity of other countries. "Free communication and exchange" seems to him an ordinance of nature; and he heaps contempt upon those "numberless bars, obstructions and imposts which all nations of Europe, and none more than England, have put upon trade." Specie he places in its true light as merely a medium of exchange. The supposed antagonism between commerce and agriculture he disposes of in a half-dozen effective sentences. He sees the place of time and distance in the discussion of economic want. He sees the value of a general level of economic equality, even while he is sceptical of its attainment. He insists upon the economic value of high wages, though he somewhat belittles the importance of wealth in the achievement of

happiness. Before Bentham, who on this
point converted Adam Smith, he knew
that the rate of interest depends upon the
supply of and demand for loans. He
insists that commerce demands a free government for its progress, pointing out,
doubtless from his abundant French experience, that an absolute government
gives to the commercial class an insuffi-
cient status of honor. He pointed out,
doubtless with France again in his mind,
the evils of an arbitrary system of taxation. "They are commonly converted,"
he says with unwonted severity, "into
punishments on industry; and also, by
their unavoidable inequality, are more
grievous, than by the real burden which
they impose." And he emphasizes his belief that the best taxes are those which,
like taxes upon luxury, press least upon
the poor.

Such insight is extraordinary enough in
the pre-Adamite epoch; but even more remarkable are his psychological foundations. The wealth of the State, he says, is
the labor of its subjects, and they work
because the wants of man are not a stated
sum, but "multiply every moment upon

him." The desire for wealth comes from the idea of pleasure; and in the *Treatise on Human Nature* he discusses with superb clarity the way in which the idea of pleasure is related at once to individual satisfaction and to that sympathy for others which is one of the roots of social existence. He points out the need for happiness in work. "The mind," he writes, "acquires new vigor, enlarges its powers and faculties, and by an assiduity in honest industry both satisfies its own appetites and prevents growth of unnatural ones"; though, like his predecessor, Francis Hutcheson, he overemphasizes the delights opened by civilization to the humbler class of men. He gives large space in his discussion to the power of will; and, indeed, one of the main advantages he ascribed to government was the compulsion it puts upon us to allow the categories of time and space a part in our calculations. He does not, being in his own life entirely free from avarice, regard the appetite for riches as man's main motive to existence; though no one was more urgent in his insistence that "the avidity of acquiring goods and possessions for

ourselves and our nearest friends is . . .
destructive of society" unless balanced by
considerations of justice. And what he
therein intended may be gathered from
the liberal notions of equality he manifested. "Every person," he wrote in a
famous passage, "if possible ought to enjoy the fruits of his labor in a full possession of all the necessaries, and many of
the conveniences of life. No one can
doubt but such an equality is most suitable to human nature, and diminishes
much less the happiness of the rich than
it adds to that of the poor." It is clear
that we have moved far from the narrow
confines of the old political arithmetic.
The theory of utility enables Hume to see
the scope of economics — the word itself
he did not know — in a more generous
perspective than at any previous time. It
would be too much to say that his grasp of
its psychological foundation enabled him
entirely to move from the limitations of
the older concept of a national prosperity
expressed only in terms of bullion to the
view of economics as a social science. But
at least he saw that economics is rooted in
the nature of men and therein he had the

secret of its true understanding. *The Wealth of Nations* would less easily have made its way had not the insight of Hume prepared the road for its reception.

What, then, and in general, is his place in the history of political thought? Clearly enough, he is not the founder of a system; his work is rather a series of pregnant hints than a consecutive account of political facts. Nor must we belittle the debt he owes to his predecessors. Much, certainly, he owed to Locke, and the full radiance of the Scottish enlightenment emerges into the day with his teaching. Francis Hutcheson gave him no small inspiration; and Hutcheson means that he was indebted to Shaftesbury. Indeed, there is much of the sturdy commonsense of the Scottish school about him, particularly perhaps in that interweaving of ethics, politics and economics, which is characteristic of the school from Hutcheson in the middle seventeenth century, to the able, if neglected, Lorimer in the nineteenth.[1]   He is entitled to be considered

[1] There are few books which show so clearly as Lorimer's *Institutes of Nations* (1872) how fully the Scottish school was in the midstream of European thought.

the real founder of utilitarianism. He
first showed how difficult it is in politics to
draw a distinction between ethical right
and men's opinion of what ought to be.
He brings to an end what Coleridge
happily called the "metapolitical school."
After him we are done with the abuse of
history to bolster up Divine Right and social contract; for there is clearly present
in his use of facts a true sense of historical
method. He put an end also to the confusion which resulted from the effort of
thinkers to erect standards of right and
wrong independent of all positive law.
He took the facts as phenomena to be explained rather than as illustrations of
some favorite thesis to be maintained in
part defiance of them. Conventional
Whiggism has no foothold after he has
done with its analysis. His utilitarianism
was the first efficient substitute for the
labored metaphysics of the contract
school; and even if he was not the first to
see through its pretensions — that is perhaps the claim of Shaftesbury — he was
the first to show the grounds of their use-
lessness. He saw that history and psychology together provide the materials for

a political philosophy. So that even if he could not himself construct it the hints at least were there.

His suggestiveness, indeed, may be measured in another fashion. The metaphysics of Burke, so far as one may use a term he would himself have repudiated, are largely those of Hume. The place of habit and of social instinct alongside of consent, the perception that reason alone will not explain political facts, the emphasis upon resistance as of last resort, the denial that allegiance is a mere contract to be presently explained, the deep respect for order — all these are, after all, the fabric from which the thought of Burke was woven. Nor is there in Bentham's defence of Utilitarianism argument in which he would have recognized novelty. Herein, at least, his proof that morality is no more than general opinion of utility constructs, in briefer form, the later arguments of Bentham, Paley and the Mills, nor can their mode of statement claim superiority to Hume's. So that on either side of his work he foreshadows the advent of the two great schools of modern political thought. His utilitarianism is the real path by which radical opinion at last found means of acceptance. His use of history is, through Burke, the ancestor of that specialized conservatism begotten of the historical method. If there is thus so much, it is, of course, tempting to ask why there is not more. If Hume has the materials why did he fail to build up a system from them? The answer seems twofold. In part it is the man himself. His genius, as his metaphysics show, lay essentially in his power of destruction; and the man who gave solipsism to philosophy was not likely to effect a new creation in politics. In part, also, the condition of the time gave little stimulus to novelty. Herein Hume was born a generation too early. Had he written when George III attempted the destruction of the system of the Revolution, and when America and France combined to raise again the basic questions of politics, he might have done therein what Adam Smith effected in his own field. But the time had not yet come; and it was left to Burke and Bentham to reap where he had sown.

CHAPTER V

I

FROM Hume until the publication of
Burke's *Present Discontents* (1770) there
is no work on English politics of the first
importance. Walpole had fallen in 1742;
but for the next fifteen years his methods
dominated the parliamentary scene. It
was only with the advent of the elder Pitt
to power that a new temper may be ob-
served, a temper quickened by what followed on the accession of George III.
Henceforward, it is not untrue to say that
the early complacency of the time was
lost; or, at least, it was no longer in the
ascendant again until the excesses of the
French Revolution enabled Burke to persuade his countrymen into that grim satisfaction with their own achievement of
which Lord Eldon is the standing model.
The signs of change are in each instance
slight, though collectively they acquire
significance. It was difficult for men to

grumble where, as under Walpole, each harvest brought them greater prosperity, or where, as under Chatham, they leaped from victory to victory. Something of the exhilaration of these years we can still catch in the letters which show the effort made by the jaded Horace Walpole to turn off with easy laughter his deep sense of pride. In the House of Commons, indeed, there is nothing, until the Wilkes case, to show that a new age has come. It is in the novels of Richardson and Fielding, the first shy hints of the romantic temper in Gray and Collins, above all in the awakening of political science, that novelty is apparent.

So far as a new current of thought can ever be referred to a single source, the French influence is the effective cause of change. Voltaire and Montesquieu had both visited England in the period of Walpole's administration, and both had been greatly influenced by what they saw. Rousseau, indeed, came later on that amazing voyage which the good-natured Hume insisted would save him from his dread of persecution, and there is evidence enough that he did not relish his experi-

ence. Yet when he came, in 1762, to publish the *Contrat Social* it was obvious that
he had drunk deeply of English thought.
The real meaning of their work to Englishmen lay in the perspective they gave to
English institutions. Naturally enough,
there was a vast difference between the
simplicity of a government where sovereignty was the monarch's will and one
in which a complex distribution of powers
was found to secure a general freedom.
The Frenchmen were amazed at the generous equality of English judicial pro-
cedure. The liberty of unlicensed print-
ing — less admirable than they accounted
it — the difference between a *Habeas
Corpus* and a *lettre de cachet,* the regular
succession of Parliaments, all these impressed them, who knew the meaning of
their absence, as a magnificent achievement. The English constitution revealed
to France an immense and unused reservoir of philosophic illustration. Even to
Englishmen itself that meaning was but
partly known. Locke's system was a
generalization from its significance at a
special crisis. Hume had partial glimpses
of its inner substance. But for most it

had become a discreet series of remedies
for particular wrongs. Its analysis as a
connected whole invigorated thought as
nothing had done since the Civil Wars had
elaborated the theory of parliamentary
sovereignty. What was more significant
was the realization of Montesquieu's import simultaneously with the effort of
George III to revive crown influence.
Montesquieu thus became the prophet of
a new race of thinkers. Rousseau's time
was not yet; though within a score of
years it was possible to see him as the rival
to Burke's conservatism.

It is worth while to linger for a moment
upon the thesis which underlies the *Esprit
des Lois* (1748). It is a commonplace
now that Montesquieu is to be regarded as
the founder of the historical method. The
present is to be explained by its ancestry.
Laws, governments, customs are not
truths absolute and universal, but relative
to the time of their origin and the country
from which they derive. It would be in-
accurate, with Rousseau on the threshold,
to say that his influence demolished the
systems of political abstraction which, at
their logical best, and in the most com-

plete unreality, are to be found in Godwin's *Political Justice;* but it is not beyond the mark to affirm that after his time
such abstract systems were on the defen-
sive. Therein, with all his faults, he had
given Burke the clue to those truths he so
profoundly saw — the sense of the State
as more than a mechanical contrivance,
the high regard for prescription, the sense
of law as the voice of past wisdom. He
was, said Burke, "the greatest genius
which has enlightened this age"; and
Burke had every reason to utter that noble
panegyric. But Montesquieu was more
than this. He emphasized legislation as
the main mechanism of social change; and
therein he is the parent of that decisive
reversal of past methods of which
Bentham first revealed the true significance. Nor had any thinker before his
time so emphasized the importance of
liberty as the true end of government;
even the placid Blackstone adopted the
utterance from him in his inaugural lec-
ture as Vinerian professor. He insisted,
too, on the danger of perversion to which
political principle lies open; a feeling
which found consistent utterance both in

the debates of the Philadelphia Convention, and in the writings of Bentham and James Mill. What, perhaps, is most immediately significant is his famous praise of the British Constitution — the secret of which he entirely misapprehended — and his discovery of its essence in the separation of powers. The short sixth chapter of his eleventh book is the real keynote of Blackstone and De Lolme. It led them to investigate, on principles of at least doubtful validity, an edifice never before described in detail. It is, when the last criticism has been made, an immense step forward from the uncouth antiquarianism of Coke's Second Institute to the neatly reticulated structure erected upon the foundations of Montesquieu's hint. That it was wrong was less important than that the attempt should have been made. The evil that men do lives after them; and few doctrines have been more noxious in their consequence than this theory of checks and balances. But Blackstone's *Commentaries* (1765–9) produced Bentham's *Fragment on Government* (1776), and with that book we enter upon the realistic study of the British Constitution.

Rousseau is in an antithetic tradition;
but just as he drew from English thinkers
so did he exercise upon the next generation an influence the more logical because
the inferences he drew were those that his
masters, with the English love of compromise, had sought to avoid. Rousseau
is the disciple of Locke; and the real difference between them is no more than a
removal of the limitations upon the power
of government which Locke had proposed.
It is a removal at every point conditioned
by the interest of the people. For Rousseau declared that the existing distribution of power in Europe was a monstrous
thing, and he made the people sovereign
that there might be no hindrance to their
achievement in the shape of sinister interest. The powers of the people thus
became their rights and herein was an unlimited sanction for innovation. It is
easy enough then to understand why such
a philosophy should have been anathema
to Burke. Rousseau's eager sympathy for
humble men, his optimistic faith in the
immediate prospect of popular power
were to Burke the symptoms of insane
delusion and their author "the great pro-

fessor and founder of the philosophy of vanity in England." But Burke forgot that the real secret of Rousseau's influence was the success of the American Revolution; and no one had done more than Burke himself to promote its cause and justify its principles. That revolution established what Europe might well consider a democracy; and its statesmen were astonished not less at the vigilance with which America guarded against the growth of autocratic government, than at the soberness with which it checked the supposed weakness of the sovereign people. America made herself independent while what was best in Europe combined in enthusiastic applause; and it seemed as though the maxims of Rousseau had been taken to heart and that a single, vigorous exertion of power could remove what deliberation was impotent to secure. Here Rousseau had a message for Great Britain which Burke at every stage denied. Nor, at the moment, was it influential except in the general impetus it gave to thought. But from the moment of its appearance it is an undercurrent of decisive importance; and while in its meta-

physical form it failed to command acceptance, in the hands of Bentham its
results were victorious. Bentham differs
from Rousseau not in the conclusions he
recommends so much as in the language in
which he clothes them. Either make a
final end of the optimism of men like
Hume and Blackstone, or the veneration
for the past which is at the root of Burke's
own teaching.

It is easy to see why thought such as
this should have given the stimulus it did.
Montesquieu came to praise the British
constitution at a time when good men were
aghast at its perversion. There was no
room in many years for revolution, but
at least there was place for hearty discontent and a seeking after new methods. Of
that temper two men so different as the
elder Pitt and Wilkes are the political
symbols. The former's rise to power upon
the floodtide of popular enthusiasm meant
nothing so much as a protest against the
cynical corruption of the previous generation. Wilkes was a sign that the populace was slowly awaking to a sense of its
own power. The French creed was too
purely logical, too obviously the outcome

of alien conditions, to fit in its entirety
the English facts; and, it must be admitted, memories of wooden shoes played
not a little part in its rejection. The
rights of man made only a partial appeal
until the miseries of Pitt's wars showed
what was involved in that rejection; and
then it was too late. But no one could
feel without being stirred the illumination
of Montesquieu; and Rousseau's questions, even if they proved unanswerable,
were stuff for thought. The work of the
forty years before the French Revolution
is nothing so much as a preparation for
Bentham. The torpor slowly passes. The
theorists build an edifice each part of
which a man whose passion is attuned to
the English nature can show to be obsolete and ugly. If the French thinkers had
conferred no other benefit, that, at least,
would have been a supreme achievement.

II

The first book to show the signs of
change came in 1757. John Brown's *Estimate of the Manners and Principles of
the Times* is largely forgotten now;

though it went through seven editions in
a year and was at once translated into
French. Brown was a clergyman, a minor
planet in the vast Warburtonian system,
who had already published a volume of
comment upon the *Characteristics* of
Shaftesbury. His book is too evidently
modelled upon Montesquieu, whom he
mentions with reverence, to make us doubt
its derivation. There is the same reliance
upon Livy and Machiavelli, the same attempt at striking generalization; though
the argument upon which Brown's conclusions are based is seldom given, perhaps because his geometric clarity of
statement impressed him as self-demon-
strative. Brown's volumes are an essay
upon the depravity of the times. He does
not deny it humanitarianism, and a still
lingering sense of freedom, but it is
steeped in corruption and displays nothing so much as a luxurious and selfish
effeminacy. He condemns the universities
out of hand, in phrases which Gibbon and
Adam Smith would not have rejected.
He deplores the decay of taste and learning. Men trifle with Hume's gay im-
pieties, and could not, if they would,

appreciate the great works of Bishop
Warburton. Politics has become nothing
save a means of promoting selfish interests. The church, the theatre, and the
arts have all of them lost their former
virtues. The neurotic temper of the times
is known to all. The nation, as was shown
in 1745, when a handful of Highlanders
penetrated without opposition to the heart
of the kingdom, has grown slack and cow-
ardly. Gambling penetrates every nook
and cranny of the upper class; the officers
of the army devote themselves to fashion;
the navy's main desire is for prize money.
Even the domestic affections are at a low
ebb; and the grand tour brings back a new
species of Italianate Englishman. The
poor, indeed, the middle class, and the
legal and medical professions, Brown
specifically exempts from this indictment.
But he emphasizes his belief that this is
unimportant. "The manners and principles of those who lead," he says, ". . .
not of those who are governed . . . will
ever determine the strength or weakness,
and therefore the continuance or dissolution of a state."

This profligacy Brown compares to the

languid vice which preceded the fall of
Carthage and of Rome; and he sees the
approaching ruin of Great Britain at the
hands of France, unless it can be cured.
So far as he has an explanation to offer,
it seems to be the fault of Walpole, and
the decay of religious sentiment. His
remedy is only Bolingbroke's Patriot
King, dressed up in the habit of the elder
Pitt, now risen to the height of power.
What mainly stirred Englishmen was the
prophecy of defeat on the morrow of the
disastrous convention of Kloster Seven;
but when Wolfe and Clive repaired that
royal humiliation Brown seems to have
died a natural death. What is more interesting than his prophecies was the evidence of a close reading of Montesquieu.
English liberty, he says, is the product of
the climate; a kind of mixture, it appears,
of fog and sullen temper. Nations inev-
itably decay, and the commercial grandeur
of England is the symptom of old age; it
means a final departure from the simplicity of nature and breeds the luxury
which kills by enervation. Brown has no
passion, and his book reads rather like Mr.
Galsworthy's *Island Pharisees* sufficiently

expurgated to be declaimed by a well-bred
clergyman in search of preferment on the
ground of attention to the evils of his
time. It describes undoubted facts, and
it shows that the era of content has gone.
But its careful periods and strangely far-
off air lack the eagerness for truth which
Rousseau put into his questions. Brown
can neither explain nor can he proffer
remedy. He sees that Pitt is somehow
significant; but when he rules out the
popular voice as devoid of all importance,
he deprives himself of the means whereby
to grasp the meaning of the power that
Pitt exerted. Nothing could prove more
strongly the exactitude of Burke's *Present Discontents*. Nothing could better
justify the savage indignation of Junius,

Hume was the friend of Montesquieu,
though twenty years his junior; and the
Esprit des Lois travelled rapidly to Scotland. There it caught the eye of Adam
Ferguson, the author of a treatise on re-
finement, and by the influence of Hume
and Adam Smith, Professor of Moral
Philosophy in the University of Edinburgh. Ferguson seems to have been im-
mensely popular in his time, and certainly

he has a skill for polished phrase, and a
genial paraphrase of other men's ideas.
His *Essay on the History of Civil Society* (1767), which in a quarter of a century went through six editions, was
thought by Helvétius superior to Montesquieu, though Hume himself, as always
the incarnation of kindness, recommended
its suppression. At least Ferguson read
enough of Montesquieu to make some
fluent generalities sound plausible. He
knows that the investigation of savage life
will throw some light upon the origins of
government. He sees the folly of generalizing easily upon the state of nature.
He insists, probably after conversation
with Adam Smith, upon the social value
of the division of functions. He does not
doubt the original equality of men. He
thinks the luxury of his age has reached
the limit of its useful growth. Property
he traces back to a parental desire to make
a better provision for children "than is
found under the promiscuous management of many copartners." Climate has
the new importance upon which Montesquieu has insisted; or, at least, as it
"ripens the pineapple and the tamarina,"

so it "inspires a degree of mildness that
can even assuage the rigours of despotical
government." The priesthood — this is
Hume — becomes a separate influence
under the sway of superstition. Liberty,
he says, "is maintained by the continued
differences and oppositions of numbers,
not by their concurring zeal in behalf of
equitable government." The hand that
can bend Ulysses' bow is certainly not
here; and this pinchbeck Montesquieu can
best be left in the obscurity into which he
has fallen. The *Esprit des Lois* took
twenty years in writing; and it needed the
immense researches of men like Savigny
before its significance could fully be
grasped. Facile popularisers of this sort
may have mollified the drawing-room;
but they did not add to political ideas.

III

A more fertile source of inquiry was to
be found among the students of constitutional law. Blackstone's *Commentaries
on the Laws of England* (1765-9) has
had ever since its first publication an authority such as Coke only before pos-

sessed. "He it is," said Bentham, "who, first of all institutional writers, has taught jurisprudence to speak the language of the Scholar and the Gentleman." Certainly, as Professor Dicey has remarked, "the book contains much real learning about our system of government." We are less concerned here with Blackstone as an antiquarian lawyer than as a student of political philosophy. Here his purpose seems obvious enough. The English constitution raised him from humble means through a Professorship at Oxford to a judgeship in the Court of Common Pleas. He had been a member of Parliament and refused the office of Solicitor-General. He had thus no reason to be dissatisfied with the conditions of his time; and the first book of the *Commentaries* is nothing so much as an attempt to explain why English constitutional law is a miracle of wisdom.

Constitutional law, as such, indeed, found no place in Blackstone's book. It creeps in under the rights of persons, where he deals with the power of king and Parliament. His treatment implies a whole philosophy. Laws are of three kinds — of nature, of God, and of the civil state. Civil law, with which alone he is concerned, is "a rule of civil conduct prescribed by the supreme power in a state, commanding what is right and prohibiting what is wrong." It is, he tells us, "called a rule to distinguish it from a compact or agreement." It derives from the sovereign power, of which the chief character is the making of laws. Society is based upon the "wants and fears" of men; and it is coeval with their origin. The idea of a state of nature "is too wild to be seriously admitted," besides being contrary to historical knowledge. Society implies government, and whatever its origins or its forms there "must be in all of them a supreme, irresistible, absolute, uncontrolled authority, in which the *jura summa imperii,* or rights of sovereignty reside." The forms of government are classified in the usual way; and the British constitution is noted as a happy mixture of them all. "The legislature of the Kingdom," Blackstone writes, "is entrusted to three powers entirely independent of each other; first the King, secondly the lords spiritual and temporal, which is an aris-

tocratical assembly of persons, chosen for
their piety, their birth, their wisdom, their
valour or their property; and, thirdly, the
House of Commons, freely chosen by the
people from among themselves, which
makes it a kind of democracy; and as this
aggregate body, actuated by different
springs and attentive to different interests, composes the British Parliament
and has the supreme disposal of everything; there can be no inconvenience attempted by either of the three branches,
but will be withstood by one of the other
two; each branch being armed with a negative power, sufficient to repel any innovation which it shall think inexpedient or
dangerous." It is in the king in Parliament that British sovereignty resides.
Eschewing the notion of an original contract, Blackstone yet thinks that all the
implications of it are secured. "The constitutional government of this island," he
says, "is so admirably tempered and compounded, that nothing can endanger or
hurt it, but destroying the equilibrium of
power between one branch of the legislature and the rest."

All this is not enough; though, as

Bentham was to show in his *Fragment on Government,* it is already far too much. "A body of nobility," such is the philosophic interpretation of the House of Lords, "is also more peculiarly necessary in our mixed and compounded constitution, in order to support the rights of both the Crown and people, by forming a barrier to withstand the encroachments of both . . . if they were confounded with the mass of the people, and like them had only a vote in electing representatives, their privileges would soon be borne down and overwhelmed by the popular torrent, which would effectually level all distinctions." "The Commons," he says further, "consist of all such men of property in the kingdom as have not seats in the House of Lords." The legal irresponsibility of the King is emphasized. "He is not only incapable of doing wrong," says Blackstone, "but even of thinking wrong; he can never mean to do an improper thing; in him is no folly or weakness," though he points out that the constitution "has allowed a latitude of supposing the contrary." The powers of the King are described in terms more suitable to the iron despotism of

William the Norman than to the backstairs corruption of George III. The
right of revolution is noted, with justice,
as belonging to the sphere of morals
rather than of law.

"Its true defect," says Professor Dicey
of the *Commentaries,* "is the hopeless
confusion both of language and of
thought introduced into the whole subject
of constitutional law by Blackstone's
habit — common to all the lawyers of his
time — of applying old and inapplicable
terms to new institutions." This is severe
enough; yet Blackstone's sins are deeper
than the criticism would suggest. He introduced into English political philosophy
that systematic attention to forms instead
of substance upon which the whole vicious
theory of checks and balances was erected.
He made no distinction between the unlimited sovereignty of law and the very
obviously limited sovereignty of reality.
He must have known that to talk of the
independence of the branches of the legislature was simple nonsense at a time when
King and peers competed for the control
of elections to the House of Commons.
His idealization of a peerage whose

typical spiritual member was Archbishop
Cornwallis and whose temporal embodiment was the Duke of Bedford would not
have deceived a schoolboy had it not provided a bulwark against improvement. It
was ridiculous to describe the Commons as
representative of property so long as
places like Manchester and Sheffield were
virtually disfranchised. His picture of
the royal prerogative was a portrait
against every detail of which what was
best in England had struggled in the preceding century and a half. He has
nothing to say of the cabinet, nothing of
ministerial responsibility, nothing of the
party system. What he did was to produce the defence of a non-existent system
which acted as a barrier to all legal, and
much political, progress in the next half-
century. He gave men material without
cause for satisfaction.

As a description of the existing government there is thus hardly an element of
Blackstone's work which could stand the
test of critical inquiry. But even worse
was its philosophy. As Bentham pointed
out, he was unaware of the distinction between society and government. The state

of nature exists, or fails to exist, with
startling inconsistency. Blackstone, in
fact, was a Lockian who knows that
Hume and Montesquieu have cut the
ground from under his master's feet, and
yet cannot understand how, without him, a
foundation is to be supplied. Locke, indeed, seems to him, as a natural conservative, to go too far, and he rejects the original contract as without basis in history;
yet contractual notions are present at
every fundamental stage of his argument.
The sovereign power, so we are told, is irresistible; and then because Blackstone is
uncertain what right is to mean, we hear
of moral limitations upon its exercise. He
speaks continually of representation without any effort to examine into the notions
it conveys. The members of society are
held to be equal; and great pains are taken
to justify existent inequalities. "The
natural foundations of sovereignty," he
writes, "are the three great requisites
. . . of wisdom, goodness and power."
Yet there is nowhere any proof in his book
that steps have been taken in the British
Constitution to associate these with the
actual exertion of authority. Nor has he

clear notions of the way in which property is to be founded. Communism, he writes in seventeenth century fashion, is the institution of the all-beneficent Creator who gave the earth to men; property comes when men occupy some special portion of the soil continuously or mix their labor with movable possessions. This is pure Locke; though the conclusions drawn by Blackstone are utterly remote from the logical result of his own premises.

The truth surely is that Blackstone had, upon all these questions, only the most confused sort of notions. He had to preface his work with some sort of philosophic theory because the conditions of the age demanded it. The one source of enlightenment when he wrote was Hume; but for some uncertain reason, perhaps his piety, Blackstone makes no reference to the great sceptic's speculations. So that he was driven back upon notions he felt to be false, without a proper realization of their falsity. His use of Montesquieu shows rather how dangerous a weapon a great idea can be in the hands of one incompetent to understand it, than the fertility it contained. The merit of Blackstone is his learning, which was substantial, his realization that the powers of law demand some classification, his dim yet constant sense that Montesquieu is right alike in searching for the roots of law in custom and in applying the historical method to his explanations. But as a thinker he was little more than an optimistic trifler, too content with the conditions of his time to question its assumptions.

De Lolme is a more interesting figure; and though, as with Blackstone, what he failed to see was even more remarkable than what he did perceive, his book has real ability and merit. De Lolme was a citizen of Geneva, who published his *Constitution of England* in 1775, after a twelve months' visit to shores sufficiently inhospitable to leave him to die in obscurity and want. His book, as he tells us in his preface, was no mean success, though he derived no profit from it. Like Blackstone, he was impressed by the necessity of obtaining a constitutional equilibrium, wherein he finds the secret of liberty. The attitude was not unnatural in one who, with his head full of Montes-

quieu, was a witness of the struggle between Junius and the King. He has, of
course, the limitation common to all
writers before Burke of thinking of government in purely mechanical terms. "It
is upon the passions of mankind," he says,
"that is, upon causes which are unalter-
able, that the action of the various parts of
a state depends. The machine may vary
as to its dimensions; but its movement and
acting springs still remain intrinsically
the same." Elsewhere he speaks of government as "a great ballet or dance in
which . . . everything depends upon the
disposition of the figures." He does not
deal, that is to say, with men as men, but
only as inert adjuncts of a machine by
which they are controlled. Such an attitude is bound to suffer from the patent
vices of all abstraction. It regards historic forces as distinct from the men related to them. Every mob, he says, must
have its Spartacus; every republic will
tend to unstability. The English avoid
these dangers by playing off the royal
power against the popular. The King's
interest is safeguarded by the division of
Parliament into two Houses, each of

which rejects the encroachment of the
other upon the executive. His power is
limited by parliamentary privilege, freedom of the press, the right of taxation and
so forth. The theory was not true; though
it represented with some accuracy the
ideals of the time.

Nor must we belittle what insight De
Lolme possessed. He saw that the early
concentration of power in the royal
hands prevented the continental type of
feudalism from developing in England;
with the result that while French nobles
were massacring each other, the English
people could unite to wrest privileges
from the superior power. He understood
that one of the mainsprings of the system
was the independence of the judges. He
realized that the party-system — he never
used the actual term — while it provides
room for men's ambitions at the same time
prevents the equation of ambition with in-
dispensability. "Woe to him," says De
Lolme, ". . . who should endeavor to
make the people believe that their fate
depends on the persevering virtue of a
single citizen." He sees the paramount
value of freedom of the press. This, as

he says, with the necessity that members
should be re-elected, "has delivered into
the hands of the people at large the exercise of the censorial power." He has
no doubt but that resistance is the remedy
whereby governmental encroachment can
be prevented; "resistance," he says, "is
the ultimate and lawful resource against
the violences of power." He points out
how real is the guarantee of liberty where
the onus of proof in criminal cases is
thrown upon the government. He regards with admiration the supremacy of
the civil over the military arm, and the
skillful way in which, contrary to French
experience, it has been found possible to
maintain a standing army without adding
to the royal power. Nor can he fail to
admire the insight which organizes "the
agitation of the popular mind," not as
"the forerunner of violent commotions"
but to "animate all parts of the state."
Therein De Lolme had grasped the real
essence of party government.

It was, of course, no more than symp-
tomatic of his time that cabinet and prime
minister should have escaped his notice.
A more serious defect was his inability,

with the Wilkes contest prominently in his notice, to see that the people had assumed a new importance. For the masses, indeed, De Lolme had no enthusiasm. "A passive share," he thought, "was the only one that could, with safety to the state, be trusted" to the humble man. "The greater part," he wrote, "of those who compose this multitude, taken up with the care oi providing for their subsistence, have neither sufficient leisure, nor even, in consequence of their imperfect education, the degree of information, requisite for functions of this kind." Such an attitude blinded him to the significance of the American conflict, which he saw unattended by its moral implications. He trusted too emphatically to the power of mechanisms to realize that institutions which allowed of such manipulation as that of George III could not be satisfactory once the people had awakened to a sense of its own power. The real social forces of the time found there no channels of activity; and the difference between De Lolme and Bagehot is the latter's power to go behind the screen of statute to the inner sources of power.

IV

The basis of revolutionary doctrine was already present in England when, in 1762, Rousseau published his *Contrat Social*. With its fundamental doctrines Locke had already made his countrymen familiar; and what was needed for the appreciation of its teaching was less a renaissance than discontent. So soon as men are dissatisfied with the traditional foundations of the State, a gospel of natural rights is certain to make its appearance. And, once the design of George III had been made familiar by his treatment of Chatham and Wilkes, the discontent did not fail to show itself. Indeed, in the year before the publication of Rousseau's book, Robert Wallace, a Scottish chaplain royal, had written in his *Various Prospects* (1761) a series of essays which are at once an anticipation of the main thesis of Malthus and a plea for the integration of social forces by which alone the mass of men could be raised from misery. In the light of later experience it is difficult not to be impressed by the modernist flavour of Wallace's attack.

He insists upon the capacity of men and
the disproportion between their potential
achievement and that which is secured by
actual society. Men are in the mass condemned to ignorance and toil; and the
lust of power sets man against his
neighbor to the profit of the rich. Wallace
traces these evils to private property and
the individualistic organization of work,
and he sees no remedy save community of
possessions and a renovated educational
system. Yet he does not conceal from
himself that it is to the interest of the
governing class to prevent a revolution
which, beneficent to the masses, would be
fatal to themselves; nor does he conceive
it possible until the fertility of men has
been reduced to the capacity of the soil.
He speculates upon the chances of a new
spirit among men, of an all-wise legislator, and of the beneficent example of
colonies upon the later Owenite model.
But his book is contemporaneous with our
own ideas rather than with the thoughts of
his generation. Nor does it seem to have
excited any general attention.

It is five years after Rousseau that we
see the first clear signs of his influence.

Naturally enough the men amongst whom the new spirit spread abroad were the Nonconformists. For more than seventy years they had been allowed existence without recognition. None had more faithfully supported the new dynasty than they; none had been paid less for their allegiance. Their utmost effort could secure only a sparing mitigation of the Test Act. All of them were Whigs, and the doctrines of Locke suited exactly their temper and their wants. There were amongst them able men in every walk of life, and they were apt to publication. Joseph Priestley, in particular, gave up with willingness to mankind what was obviously meant for chemical science. A few years previously Brown of the *Estimate* had submitted a scheme for national education, in which the essential principle was Church control. Priestley had answered him, and was encouraged by friends to expand his argument into a general treatise. His *Essay on the First Principles of Government* appeared in 1768; and, if for nothing else, it would be noteworthy because it was therein that the significance of the "greatest happiness principle" first

flashed across Bentham's mind. But the
book shows more than this. "I had
placed," says Priestley with due modesty,
"the foundation of some of the most valuable interests of mankind on a broader and
firmer basis than Mr. Locke"; and the
breadth and firmness are Rousseau's contribution.

Certainly we herein meet new elements.
On the very threshold of the book we meet
the dogma of the perfectibility of man.
"Whatever," Priestley rhapsodizes, "was
the beginning of this world, the end will
be glorious and paradisaical, beyond what
our imaginations can now conceive."
"The instrument of this progress . . .
towards this glorious state" is government; though a little later we are to find
that the main business of government is
noninterference. Men are all equal, and
their natural rights are indefeasible. Government must be restrained in the interests of liberty. No man can be governed without his consent; for government
is founded upon a contract by which civil
liberty is surrendered in exchange for a
power to share in public decisions. It
thus follows that the people must be sov-

ereign, and interference with their natural
rights will justify resistance. Every government, he says, is "in its original principles, and antecedent to its present form
an equal republic"; wherefore, of course,
it follows that we must restore to men the
equality they have lost. And, equally, of
course, this would bestow upon the Nonconformists their full citizenship; for
Warburton's *Alliance,* to attack which
Priestley exhausts all the resources of his
ingenuity, has been one of the main instruments in their degradation. "Un-
bounded liberty in matters of religion,"
which means the abolition of the Establishment, promises to be "very favorable
to the best interests of mankind."

So far the book might well be called an
edition of Rousseau for English Nonconformists; but there are divergences of
import. It can never be forgotten in the
history of political ideas that the alliance
of Church and State made Nonconformists suspicious of government interference.
Their original desire to be left unimpeded
was soon exalted into a definite theory;
and since political conditions had confined
them so largely to trade none felt as they

did the hampering influence of State-restrictions. The result has been a great difficulty in making liberal doctrines in England realize, until after 1870, the organic nature of the State. It remains for them almost entirely a police institution which, once it aims at the realization of right, usurps a function far better performed by individuals. There is no sense of the community; all that exists is a sum of private sentiments. "Civil liberty," says Priestley, "has been greatly impaired by an abuse of the maxim that the joint understanding of all the members of a State, properly collected, must be preferable to that of individuals; and consequently that the more the cases are in which mankind are governed by this united reason of the whole community, so much the better; whereas, in truth, the greater part of human actions are of such a nature, that more inconvenience would follow from their being fixed by laws than from their being left to every man's arbitrary will." If my neighbor assaults me, he suggests, I may usefully call in the police; but where the object is the discovery of truth, the means of education,

the method of religious belief, individual
initiative is superior to State action. The
latter produces an uniform result "incompatible with the spirit of discovery." Nor
is such attempt at uniform conditions just
to posterity; men have no natural right to
judge for the future. Men are too ignorant to fix their own ideas as the basis
of all action.

Priestley could not escape entirely the
bondage of past tradition; and the metaphysics which Bentham abhorred are
scattered broadcast over his pages.
Nevertheless the basis upon which he defended his ideas was a utilitarianism
hardly less complete than that which
Bentham made the instrument of revolution. "Regard to the general good," he
says, "is the main method by which
natural rights are to be defended." "The
good and happiness of the members, that
is, the majority of the members of any
State, is the great standard by which
everything relating to that state must
finally be determined." In substance,
that is to say, if not completely in theory,
we pass with Priestley from arguments of
right to those of expediency. His chief

attack upon religious legislation is simi-
larly based upon considerations of policy.
His view of the individual as a never-end-
ing source of fruitful innovation antici-
pates all the later Benthamite arguments
about the well-spring of individual
energy. Interference and stagnation are
equated in exactly similar fashion to
Adam Smith and his followers. Priestley,
of course, was inconsistent in urging at
the outset that government is the chief instrument of progress; but what he seems
to mean is less that government has the
future in its hands than that government
action may well be decisive for good or
evil. Typical, too, of the later Benthamism is his glorification of reason as
the great key which is to unlock all doors.
That is, of course, natural in a scientist
who had himself made discoveries of vital
import; but it was characteristic also of a
school which scanned a limitless horizon
with serene confidence in a future of un-
bounded good. Even if it be said that
Priestley has all the vices of that rationalism which, as with Bentham, over-
simplifies every problem it encounters, it
is yet adequate to retort that a confidence

in the energies of men was better than the complacent stagnation of the previous age.

It is difficult to measure the precise influence that Priestley exerted; certainly among Nonconformists it cannot have been small. Dr. Richard Price is a lesser figure; and much of the standing he might have had has been obliterated by two unfortunate incidents. His sinking-fund scheme was taken up by the younger Pitt, and proved, though the latter believed in it to the last, to be founded upon an arithmetical fallacy which did not sit well upon a fellow of the Royal Society. His sermon on the French Revolution provoked the *Reflections* of Burke; and, though much of the right was on the side of Price, it can hardly be said that he survived Burke's onslaught. Yet he was a considerable figure in his day, and he shows, like Priestley, how deep-rooted was the English revolutionary temper. He has not, indeed, Priestley's superb optimism; for the rigid *a priori* morality of which he was the somewhat muddled defender was less favorable to a confidence in reason. He had a good deal of John Brown's fear that

luxury was the seed of English degenera-
tion; the proof of which he saw in the decline of the population. His figures, in
fact, were false; but they were unessential
to the general thesis he had to make.

Price, like Priestley a leading Nonconformist, was stirred to print by the American Revolution; and if his views were not
widely popular, his *Observations on the
Nature of Civil Liberty* (1776) attained
its eighth edition within a decade. This,
with its supplement *Additional Observations* (1777), presents a perfectly coherent
theory. Nor is their ancestry concealed.
They represent the tradition of Locke,
modified by the importations of Rousseau.
Price owes much to Priestley and to
Hume, and he takes sentences from Montesquieu where they aid him. But he has
little or nothing of Priestley's utilitarianism and the whole argument is upon
the abstract basis of right. Liberty means
self-government, and self-government
means the right of every man to be his
own legislator. Price, with strict logic,
follows out this doctrine to its last consequence. Taxes become "free gifts for
public services"; laws are "particular pro-

visions or regulations established by Common Consent for gaining protection and safety"; magistrates are "trustees or deputies for carrying these regulations into execution." And almost in the words of Rousseau, Price goes on to admit that liberty, "in its most perfect degree, can be enjoyed only in small states where every independent agent is capable of giving his suffrage in person and of being chosen into public offices." He knows that large States are inevitable, though he thinks that representation may be made so adequate as to minimize the sacrifice of liberty involved.

But the limitation upon government is everywhere emphasized. "Government," he says, ". . . is in the very nature of it a trust; and all its powers a Delegation for particular ends." He rejects the theory of parliamentary sovereignty as incompatible with self-government; if the Parliament, for instance, prolonged its life, it would betray its constituents and dissolve itself. "If omnipotence," he writes, "can with any sense be ascribed to a legislature, it must be lodged where all legislative authority originates; that is, in

the People." Such a system is alone compatible with the ends of government, since
it cannot be supposed that men "combine
into communities and institute government" for self-enslavement. Nor is any
other political system "consistent with the
natural equality of mankind"; by which
Price means that no man "is constituted
by the author of nature the vassal or subject of another, or has any right to give
law to him, or, without his consent, to take
away any part of his property or to
abridge him of his liberty." From all of
which it is concluded that liberty is inalienable; and a people which has lost it
"must have a right to emancipate themselves as soon as they can." The aptness
of the argument to the American situation
is obvious enough; and nowhere is Price
more happy or more formidable than
when he applies his precepts to phrases
like "the unity of the empire" and the
"honor of the kingdom" which were so
freely used to cover up the inevitable results of George's obstinacy.

The *Essay on the Right of Property in
Land* (1781) of William Ogilvie deserves
at least a passing notice. The author, who

published his book anonymously, was a Professor of Latin in the University of Aberdeen and an agriculturist of some success. His own career was distinctly honorable. The teacher of Sir James Mackintosh, he had a high reputation as a classical scholar and deserves to be remembered for his effort to reform a college which had practically ceased to perform its proper academic functions. His book is virtually an essay upon the natural right of men to the soil. He does not doubt that the distress of the times is due to the land monopoly. The earth being given to men in common, its invasion by private ownership is a dangerous perversion. Men have the right to the full product of their labor; but the privileges of the landowner prevent the enjoyment of that right. The primary duty of every State is the increase of public happiness; and the happiest nation is that which has the greatest number of free and independent cultivators. But governments attend rather to the interest of the higher classes, even while they hold out the protection of the common people as the main pretext of their authority.

The result is their maintenance of land-
monopoly even though it affects the prime
material of all essential industries, prevents the growth of population, and
makes the rich wealthier at the expense of
the poor. It breeds oppression and ignorance, and poisons improvement by
preventing individual initiative. He
points out how a nation is dominated by
its landlords, and how they have consistently evaded the fiscal burdens they
should bear. Only in a return to a nation
of freeholders can Ogilvie see the real
source of an increase in happiness.

Such criticism is revolutionary enough,
though when he comes to speak of actual
changes, he had little more to propose
than a system of peasant proprietorship.
What is striking in the book is its sense of
great, impending changes, its thorough
grasp of the principle of utility, its realization of the immense agricultural improvement that is possible if the landed
system can be so changed as to bring into
play the impulses of humble men. He
sees clearly enough that wealth dominates the State; and his interpretation of
history is throughout economic. Ogilvie

is one of the first of those agrarian Socialists who, chiefly through Spence and
Paine, are responsible for a special current of their own in the great tide of protest against the unjust situation of labor.
Like them, he builds his system upon
natural rights; though, unlike them, his
natural rights are defended by expediency
and in a style that is always clear and
logical. The book itself has rather a curious history. At its appearance, it seems
to have excited no notice of any kind.
Mackintosh knew of its authorship; for
he warned its author against the amiable
delusion that its excellence would persuade the British government to force a
system of peasant proprietorship upon the
East India Company. Reprinted in 1838
as the work of John Ogilby, it was intended to instruct the Chartists in the
secret of their oppression; and therein it
may well have contributed to the tragi-
comic land-scheme of Feargus O'Connor.
In 1891 the problem of the land was again
eagerly debated under the stimulus of Mr.
Henry George; and a patriotic Scotch-
man published the book with biographical
notes that constitute one of the most

amazing curiosities in English political literature.

V

Against the school of Rousseau's English disciples it is comparatively easy to multiply criticisms. They lacked any historic sense. Government, for them, was simply an instrument which was made and unmade at the volition of men. How complex were its psychological foundations they had no conception; with the single factor of consent they could explain the most marvellous edifice of any time. They were buried beneath a mountain of metaphysical right which they never related to legal facts or to political possibility. They pursued relentlessly the logical conclusions of the doctrines they abhorred without being willing carefully to investigate the results to which their own doctrines in logic led. They overestimated the extent to which men are willing to occupy themselves with political affairs. They made no proper allowance for the protective armour each social system must acquire by the mere force of prescription. Nor is

there sufficient allowance in their attitude
for those limiting conditions of circumstance of which every statesman must of
necessity take account. They occupy
themselves, that is to say, so completely
with *staatslehre* that they do not admit the
mollifying influence of *politik*. They
search for principles of universal right,
without the perception that a right which
is to be universal must necessarily be so
general in character as to be useless in its
application.

Yet such defects must not blind us to
the general rightness of their insight.
They were protesting against a system
strongly upheld on grounds which now
appear to have been simply indefensible.
The business of government had been
made the private possession of a privileged class; and eagerness for desirable
change was, in the mass, absent from the
minds of most men engaged in its direction. The loss of America, the heartless
treatment of Ireland, the unconstitutional
practices in the Wilkes affair, the
heightening of corruption undertaken by
Henry Fox and North at the direct instance of the king, had blinded the eyes of

most to the fact that principle is a vital
part of policy. The revolutionists re-
called men to the need of explaining, no
less than carrying on, the government of
the Crown.   They represented the new
sense of power felt by elements of which
the importance had been forgotten in the
sordid intrigues of the previous half-century.   Their emphasis upon government
as in its nature a public trust was at least
accompanied by a useful reminder that,
after all, ultimate power must rest upon
the side of the governed. For twenty
years Whigs and Tories alike carried on
political controversy as though no public
opinion existed outside the small circle of
the aristocracy. The mob which made
Wilkes its idol was, in a blind and unconscious way, enforcing the lesson that Price
and Priestley had in mind. For the moment, they were unsuccessful.   Cartwright, with his Constitutional Societies,
might capture the support of an eccentric
peer like the Duke of Richmond; but the
vast majority remained, if irritated, un-
convinced. It needed the realization that
the new doctrines were part of a vaster
synthesis which swept within its purview

the fortunes of Europe and America before they would give serious heed; and
even then they met antagonism with
nothing save oppression and hate. Yet
the doctrines remained; for thought, after
all, is killed by reasoned answer alone.
And when the first gusts of war and revolution had passed, the cause for which they
stood was found to have permeated all
classes save that which had all to lose by
learning.

We must not, however, commit the
error of thinking of Price and Priestley as
representing more than an important seg-
ment of opinion. The opposition to their
theories was not less articulate than their
own defence of them. Some, like Burke,
desired a purification of the existing system; others, like Dr. Johnson, had no sort
of sympathy with new-fangled ideas. One
thinker, at least, deserves some mention
less for the inherent value of what he had
to say, than for the nature of the opinions
he expounded. Josiah Tucker, the Dean
of Gloucester, has a reputation alike in
political and economic enquiry. He represents the sturdy nationalism of Arbuth-
not's *John Bull*, the unreasoned preju-

dice against all foreigners, the hatred of
all metaphysics as inconsistent with
common sense, the desire to let things be
on the ground that the effort after change
is worse than the evil of which men complain. His *Treatise on Civil Government*
(1781) is in many ways a delightful book,
bluff, hardy, full of common sense, with,
at times, a quaint humor that is all its own.
He had really two objects in view; to deal,
in the first place, faithfully with the
American problem, and, in the second, to
explode the new bubble of Rousseau's followers. The second point takes the form
of an examination of Locke, to whom, as
Tucker shrewdly saw, the theories of the
school may trace their ancestry. He an-
alyses the theory of consent in such
fashion as to show that if its adherents
could be persuaded to be logical, they
would have to admit themselves an-
archists. He has no sympathy with the
state of nature; the noble savage, on investigation, turns out to be a barbaric
creature with a club and scalping knife.
Government, he does not doubt, is a trust,
or, as he prefers, somewhat oddly, to call
it, a quasi-contract; but that does not mean

that the actual governors can be dismissed
when any eccentric happens to take exception to their views. He has no sympathy with parliamentary reform. Give
the mob an increase of power, he says, and
nothing is to be expected but outrage and
violence. He thinks the constitution very
well as it is, and those who preach the evils
of corruption ought to prove their charges
instead of blasphemously asserting that
the voice of the people is the voice of God.

Upon America Tucker has doctrines all
his own. He does not doubt that the
Americans deserve the worst epithets that
can be showered upon them. Their right
to self-government he denied as stoutly as
ever George III himself could have desired. But not for one moment would he
fight them to compel their return to
British allegiance. If the American colonies want to go, let them by all means
cut adrift. They are only a useless source
of expenditure. The trade they represent
does not depend upon allegiance but upon
wants that England can supply if she
keeps shop in the proper way, if, that is,
she makes it to their interest to buy in her
market. Indeed, colonies of all kinds

seem to him quite useless. They ever are, he says, and ever were, "a drain to and an incumbrance on the Mother-country, requiring perpetual and expensive nursing in their infancy, and becoming headstrong and ungovernable in proportion as they grow up." All wise relations depend upon self-interest, and that needs no compulsion. If Gibraltar and Port Mahon and the rest were given up, the result would be "multitudes of places . . . abolished, jobs and contracts effectually prevented, millions of money saved, universal industry encouraged, and the influence of the Crown reduced to that mediocrity it ought to have." Here is pure Manchesterism half-a-century before its time; and one can imagine the good Dean crustily explaining his notions to the merchants of Bristol who had just rejected Edmund Burke for advocating free trade with Ireland.

No word on Toryism would be complete without mention of Dr. Johnson. Here, indeed, we meet less with opinion than with a set of gloomy prejudices, acceptable only because of the stout honesty of the source from which they come. He

thought life a poor thing at the best and
took a low view of human nature. "The
notion of liberty," he told the faithful
Boswell, "amuses the people of England
and helps to keep off the *tedium vitae*."
The idea of a society properly organized
into ranks and societies he always es-
teemed highly. "I am a friend to subordination," he said, "as most conducive
to the happiness of society." He was a
Jacobite and Tory to the end. Whiggism
was the offspring of the devil, the "negation of all principle"; and he seems to have
implied that it led to atheism, which he
regarded as the worst of sins. He did not
believe in the honesty of republicans; they
levelled down, but were never inclined to
level up. Men, he felt, had a part to act
in society, and their business was to fulfil
their allotted station. Rousseau was a
very bad man: "I would sooner sign a
sentence for his transportation than that
of any fellow who has gone from the Old
Bailey these many years." Political liberty was worthless; the only thing worth
while was freedom in private concerns.
He blessed the government in the case of
general warrants and thought the power

of the Crown too small. Toleration he
considered due to an inapt distinction between freedom to think and freedom to
talk, and any magistrate "while he thinks
himself right . . . ought to enforce what
he thinks." The American revolt he ascribed to selfish faction; and in his *Taxation no Tyranny* (1775) he defended the
British government root and branch upon
his favorite ground of the necessity of
subordination. He was willing, he said,
to love all mankind except an American.

Yet Dr. Johnson was the friend of
Burke, and he found pleasure in an acquaintance with Wilkes. Nor, in all his
admiration for rank and fortune, is there
a single element of meanness. The man
who wrote the letter to Lord Chesterfield
need never fear the charge of abasement.
He knew that there was "a remedy in
human nature that will keep us safe under
every form of government." He defined
a courtier in the *Idler* as one "whose business it is to watch the looks of a being
weak and foolish as himself." Much of
what he felt was in part a revolt against
the sentimental aspect of contemporary
liberalism, in part a sturdy contempt for

the talk of degeneracy that men such as
Brown had made popular. There is, indeed, in all his political observations a
strong sense of the virtue of order, and a
perception that the radicalism of the time
was too abstract to provide an adequate
basis for government. Here, as elsewhere,
Johnson hated all speculation which raised
the fundamental questions. What he did
not see was the important truth that in no
age are fundamental questions raised save
where the body politic is diseased. Rousseau and Voltaire, even Priestley and
Price, require something more for answer
than unreasoned prejudice. Johnson's
attitude would have been admirable where
there were no questions to debate; but
where Pelham ruled, or Grenville, or
North, it had nothing to contribute.
Thought, after all, is the one certain
weapon of utility in a different and complex world; and it was because the age
refused to look it in the face that it invited the approach of revolution.

CHAPTER VI

BURKE

I

IT is the special merit of the English constitutional system that the king stands outside the categories of political conflict. He is the dignified emollient of an organized quarrel which, at least in theory, is due to the clash of antagonistic principle. The merit, indeed, is largely accidental; and we shall miss the real fashion in which it came to be established unless we remark the vicissitudes through which it has passed. The foreign birth of the first two Hanoverians, the insistent widowhood of Queen Victoria, these rather than deliberate foresight have secured the elevated nullification of the Crown. Yet the first twenty-five years of George III's reign represent the deliberate effort of an obstinate man to stem the progress of fifty years and secure once more the balance of power. Nor was the effort defeated without a struggle which went to the root of constitutional principle.

And George III attempted the realization of his ambition at a time highly favorable to its success. Party government had lost much credit during Walpole's administration. Men like Bolingbroke, Carteret and the elder Pitt were all of them dissatisfied with a system which depended for its existence upon the exclusion of able men from power. A generation of corrupt practice and the final defeat of Stuart hopes had already deprived the Whigs of any special hold on their past ideals. They were divided already into factions the purpose of which was no more than the avid pursuit of place and pension. Government by connection proved itself irreconcilable with good government. But it showed also that once corruption was centralized there was no limit to its influence, granted only the absence of great questions. When George III transferred that organization from the office of the minister to his own court, there was already a tolerable certainty of his success. For more than forty years the Tories had

been excluded from office; and they were
more than eager to sell their support. The
Church had become the creature of the
State. The drift of opinion in continental
Europe was towards benevolent despotism. The narrow, obstinate and un-
generous mind of George had been fed on
high notions of the power he might exert.
He had been taught the kingship of Bolingbroke's glowing picture; and a reading
in manuscript of the seventh chapter of
Blackstone's first book can only have confirmed the ideals he found there. Nor
was it obvious that a genuine kingship
would have been worse than the oligarchy
of the great Whig families.

What made it worse, and finally impossible, was the character of the king.
The pathetic circumstances of his old age
have combined somewhat to obscure the
viciousness of his maturity. He was ex-
cessively ignorant and as obstinate as arbitrary. He trusted no one but himself,
and he totally misunderstood the true nature of his office. There is no question
which arose in the first forty years of his
reign in which he was not upon the wrong
side and proud of his error. He was

wrong about Wilkes, wrong about
America, wrong about Ireland, wrong
about France. He demanded servants instead of ministers. He attacked every
measure for the purification of the political system. He supported the Slave
trade and he opposed the repeal of the
Test Act. He prevented the grant of
Catholic emancipation at the one moment
when it might have genuinely healed the
wounds of Ireland. He destroyed by his
perverse creations the value of the House
of Lords as a legislative assembly. He
was clearly determined to make his will
the criterion of policy; and his design
might have succeeded had his ability and
temper been proportionate to its greatness. It was not likely that the mass of
men would have seen with regret the destruction of the aristocratic monopoly in
politics. The elder Pitt might well have
based a ministry of the court upon a broad
bottom of popularity. The House of
Commons, as the event proved, could be
as subservient to the king as to his
minister.

Yet the design failed; and it failed because, with characteristic stupidity, the

king did not know the proper instruments
for his purpose. Whatever he touched he
mismanaged. He aroused the suspicion of
the people by enforcing the resignation of
the elder Pitt. In the Wilkes affair he
threw the clearest light of the century
upon the true nature of the House of
Commons. His own system of proscription restored to the Whig party not a little
of the idealism it had lost; and Burke
came to supply them with a philosophy.
Chatham remained the idol of the people
despite his hatred. He raised Wilkes to
be the champion of representative government and of personal liberty. He lost
America and it was not his fault that Ireland was retained. The early popularity
he received he never recovered until increasing years and madness had made him
too pathetic for dislike. The real result
of his attempt was to compel attention
once again to the foundations of politics;
and George's effort, in the light of his
immense failures, could not, in the nature
of things, survive that analysis.

Not, of course, that George ever lacked
defenders. As early as 1761, the old rival
of Walpole, Pulteney, whom a peerage

had condemned to obsolescence, published his *Seasonable Hints from an Honest Man on the new Reign.* Pulteney urged the sovereign no longer to be content with the "shadow of royalty." He should use his "legal prerogatives" to check "the illegal claims of factious oligarchy." Government had become the private possession of a few powerful men. The king was but a puppet in leading strings. The basis of government should be widened, for every honest man was aware that distinctions of party were now merely nominal. The Tories should be admitted to place. They were now friendly to the accession and they no longer boasted their hostility to dissent. They knew that Toleration and the Establishment were of the essence of the Constitution. Were once the Whig oligarchy overthrown, corruption would cease and Parliament could no longer hope to dominate the kingdom. "The ministers," he said, "will depend on the Crown not the Crown on ministers" if George but showed "his resolution to break all factitious connections and confederacies." The tone is Bolingbroke's, and it was the lesson George had insistently heard from early youth. How sinister was the advice, men did not see until the elder Pitt was in political·exile, with Wilkes an outlaw, and general warrants threatening the whole basis of past liberties.

The first writer who pointed out in unmistakable terms the meaning of the new synthesis was Junius. That his anonymity concealed the malignant talent of Sir Philip Francis seems now beyond denial. Junius, indeed, can hardly claim a place in the history of political ideas. His genius lay not in the discussion of principle but the dissection of personality. His power lay in his style and the knowledge that enabled him to inform the general public of facts which were the private possession of the inner political circle. His mind was narrow and pedantic. He stood with Grenville on American taxation; and he maintained without perceiving what it meant that a nomination borough was a freehold beyond the competence of the legislature to abolish. He was never generous, always abusive, and truth did not enter into his calculations. But he saw with unsurpassed clearness the nature of the issue and he was a powerful instrument in the discomfiture of the king. He.won a new audience for political conflict and that audience was the unenfranchised populace of England. His letters, moreover, appearing as they did in the daily journals gave the press a significance in politics which it has never lost. He made the significance of George's effort known to the mass of men at a time when no other means of information was at hand. The opposition was divided; the king's friends were in a vast majority; the publication of debates was all but impossible. English government was a secret conflict in which the entrance of spectators was forbidden even though they were the subjects of debate. It was the glory of Junius that he destroyed that system. Not even the combined influence of the Crown and Commons, not even Lord Mansfield's doctrine of the law of libel, could break the power of his vituperation and Wilkes' courage. Bad men have sometimes been the instruments of noble destiny; and there are few more curious episodes in English history than the result of this alliance between revengeful hate and insolent ambition.

II

Yet, in the long run, the real weapon which defeated George was the ideas of Edmund Burke; for he gave to the political conflict its real place in philosophy. There is no immortality save in ideas; and it was Burke who gave a permanent form to the debate in which he was the liberal protagonist. His career is illustrative at once of the merits and defects of English politics in the eighteenth century. The son of an Irish Protestant lawyer and a Catholic mother, he served, after learning what Trinity College, Dublin, could offer him, a long apprenticeship to politics in the upper part of Grub Street. The story that he applied, along with Hume, for Adam Smith's chair at Glasgow seems apocryphal; though the *Dissertation on the Sublime and the Beautiful* (1756) shows his singular fitness for the studies that Hutcheson had made the special possession of the Scottish school. It was in Grub Street that he appears to have attained that amazing amount of varied yet profound knowledge which made him without equal in the House of Commons.

His earliest production was a *Vindication of Natural Society* (1756), written in the manner of Lord Bolingbroke, and successful enough in its imitative satire not only to deceive its immediate public, but also to become the basis of Godwin's *Political Justice*. After a vain attempt to serve in Ireland with "Single-Speech" Hamilton, he became the private secretary to Lord Rockingham, the leader of the one section of the Whig party to which an honorable record still remained. That connection secured for him a seat in Parliament at the comparatively late age of thirty-six; and henceforward, until his death in 1797, he was among its leading members. His intellectual pre-eminence, indeed, seems from the very outset to have been recognized on all hands; though he was still, in the eyes of the system, enough of an outsider to be given, in the short months during which he held office, the minor office of Paymaster-General, without a seat in the Cabinet. The man of whom all England was the political pupil was denied without discussion a place at the council board. Yet when Fox is little more than a memory of great lovableness and Pitt a marvellous youth of apt quotations, Burke has endured as the permanent manual of political wisdom without which statesmen are as sailors on an uncharted sea.

For it has been the singular good fortune of Burke not merely to obtain acceptance as the apostle of philosophic conservatism, but to give deep comfort to men of liberal temper. He is, indeed, a singularly lovable figure. "His stream of mind is perpetual," said Johnson; and Goldsmith has told us how he wound his way into a subject like a serpent. Macaulay thought him the greatest man since Milton, Lord Morley the "greatest master of civil wisdom in our tongue." "No English writer," says Sir Leslie Stephen, "has received or has deserved more splendid panegyrics." Even when the last criticism has been made, detraction from these estimates is impossible. It is easy to show how irritable and violent was his temperament. There is evidence and to spare of the way in which he allowed the spirit of party to cloud his judgment. His relations with Lord Chatham give lamentable proof of the violence of his personal antipathies. As an orator, his speeches are often turgid, wanting in self-control, and full of those ample digressions in which Mr. Gladstone delighted to obscure his principles. Yet the irritation did not conceal a magnificent loyalty to his friends, and it was in his days of comparative poverty that he shared his means with Barry and with Crabbe. His alliance with Fox is the classic partnership in English politics, unmarried, even enriched, by the tragedy of its close. He was never guilty of mean ambition. He thought of nothing save the public welfare. No man has ever more consistently devoted his energies to the service of the nation with less regard for personal advancement. No English statesman has ever more firmly moved amid a mass of details to the principle they involve.

He was a member of no school of thought, and there is no influence to whom his outlook can be directly traced. His politics, indeed, bear upon their face the preoccupation with the immediate problems of the House of Commons. Yet through them all the principles that

emerge form a consistent whole. Nor is
this all. He hated oppression with all the
passion of a generous moral nature. He
cared for the good as he saw it with a
steadfastness which Bright and Cobden
only can claim to challenge. What he had
to say he said in sentences which form the
maxims of administrative wisdom. His
horizon reached from London out to
India and America; and he cared as
deeply for the Indian ryot's wrongs as
for the iniquities of English policy to Ireland. With less width of mind than
Hume and less intensity of gaze than
Adam Smith, he yet had a width and intensity which, fused with his own imagina-
tive sympathy, gave him more insight
than either. He had an unerring eye for
the eternal principles of politics. He
knew that ideals must be harnessed to an
Act of Parliament if they are not to cease
their influence. Admitting while he did
that politics must rest upon expediency,
he never failed to find good reason why
expediency should be identified with what
he saw as right. It is a stainless and a
splendid record. There are men in English politics to whom a greater immediate

influence may be ascribed, just as in political philosophy he cannot claim the persistent inspiration of Hobbes and Locke.
But in that middle ground between the
facts and speculation his supremacy is un-
approached. There had been nothing like
him before in English politics; and in continental politics Royer Collard alone has
something of his moral fibre, though his
practical insight was far less profound.
Hamilton had Burke's full grasp of political wisdom, but he lacked his moral
elevation. So that he remains a figure of
uniqueness. He may, as Goldsmith said,
have expended upon his party talents that
should have illuminated the universal aspect of the State. Yet there is no question with which he dealt that he did not
leave the richer for his enquiry.

III

The liberalism of Burke is most apparent in his handling of the immediate
issues of the age. Upon Ireland,
America and India, he was at every point
upon the side of the future. Where constitutional reform was in debate no man

saw more clearly than he the evils that needed remedy; though, to a later generation, his own schemes bear the mark of timid conservatism. In the last decade of his life he encountered the greatest cataclysm unloosed upon Europe since the Reformation, and it is not too much to say that at every point he missed the essence of its meaning. Yet even upon France and the English Constitution he was full of practical sagacity. Had his warning been uttered without the fury of hate that accompanied it, he might well have guided the forces of the Revolution into channels that would have left no space for the military dictatorship he so marvellously foresaw. Had he perceived the real evils of the aristocratic monopoly against which he so eloquently inveighed, forty barren years might well have been a fruitful epoch of wise and continuous reform. But Burke was not a democrat, and, at bottom, he had little regard for that popular sense of right which, upon occasion, he was ready to praise. What impressed him was less the evils of the constitution than its possibilities, could the defects quite alien from its nature but

be pruned away. Moments, indeed, there
are of a deeper vision, and it is not untrue
to say that the best answer to Burke's conservatism is to be found in his own pages.
But he was too much the apostle of order
to watch with calm the struggles involved
in the overthrow of privilege. He had
too much the sense of a Divine Providence
taking thought for the welfare of men to
interfere with violence in his handiwork.
The tinge of caution is never absent, even
from his most liberal moments; and he
was willing to endure great evil if it
seemed dangerous to estimate the cost of
change.

His American speeches are the true
text-book for colonial administration. He
put aside the empty plea of right which
satisfied legal pedants like George Grenville. What moved him was the tragic
fashion in which men clung to the shadow
of a power they could not maintain instead of searching for the roots of freedom. He never concealed from himself
that the success of America was bound up
with the maintenance of English liberties.
"Armies," he said many years later, "first
victorious over Englishmen, in a conflict

for English constitutional rights and
privileges, and afterwards habituated
(though in America) to keep an English
people in a state of abject subjection,
would prove fatal in the end to the liberties of England itself." He had firm
hold of that insidious danger which belittles freedom itself in the interest of cur-
tailing some special desire. "In order to
prove that the Americans have no right to
their liberties," he said in the famous
Speech on Conciliation with America
(1775), "we are every day endeavoring to
subvert the maxims which preserve the
whole spirit of our own." The way for
the later despotism of the younger Pitt,
was, as Burke saw, prepared by those who
persuaded Englishmen of the paltry character of the American contest. His own
receipt was sounder. In the *Speech on
American Taxation* (1774) he had riddled
the view that the fiscal methods of Lord
North were likely to succeed. The true
method was to find a way of peace. "No-
body shall persuade me," he told a hostile
House of Commons, "when a whole
people are concerned that acts of lenity
are not means of conciliation." "Mag-

nanimity in politics," he said in the next year, "is not seldom the truest wisdom; and a great empire and little minds go ill together." He did not know, in the most superb of all his maxims, how to draw up an indictment against a whole people. He would win the colonies by binding them to England with the ties of freedom. "The question with me," he said, "is not whether you have a right to render your people miserable, but whether it is not your interest to make them happy." The problem, in fact, was one not of abstract right but of expediency; and nothing could be lost by satisfying American desire. Save for Johnson and Gibbon, that was apparent to every first-class mind in England. But the obstinate king prevailed; and Burke's great protest remained no more than material for the legislation of the future. Yet it was something that ninety years after his speech the British North America Act should have given his dreams full substance.

Ireland had always a place apart in Burke's affections, and when he first entered the House of Commons he admitted that uppermost in his thoughts was the

desire to assist its freedom. He saw that
here, as in America, no man will be argued
into slavery. A government which defied
the fundamental impulses of men was
bound to court disaster. How could it
seek security where it defied the desires of
the vast majority of its subjects? Why
is the Irish Catholic to have less justice
than the Catholic of Quebec or the Indian
Mohammedan? The system of Protestant control, he said in the *Letter to Sir
Hercules Langrishe* (1792), was "well
fitted for the oppression, impoverishment
and degradation of a people, and the de-
basement in them of human nature itself."
The Catholics paid their taxes; they
served with glory in the army and navy.
Yet they were denied a share in the commonwealth. "Common sense," he said,
"and common justice dictate . . . some
sort of compensation to a people for their
slavery." The British Constitution was
not made "for great, general and pro-
scriptive exclusions; sooner or later it will
destroy them, or they will destroy the constitution." The argument that the body
of Catholics was prone to sedition was no
reason to oppress them. "No man will

assert seriously," he said, "that when
people are of a turbulent spirit the best
way to keep them in order is to furnish
them with something to complain of."
The advantages of subjects were, as he
urged, their right; and a wise government
would regard "all their reasonable wishes
as so many claims." To neglect them was
to have a nation full of uneasiness; and the
end was bound to be disaster.

There is nothing more noble in Burke's
career than his long attempt to mitigate
the evils of Company rule in India. Research may well have shown that in some
details he pressed the case too far; yet
nothing has so far come to light to cast
doubt upon the principles he there maintained. He was the first English statesman fully to understand the moral import
of the problem of subject races; and if he
did not make impossible the Joseph Sed-
leys of the future, at least he flung an
eternal challenge to their malignant complacency. He did not ask the abandon-
ment of British dominion in India, though
he may have doubted the wisdom of its
conquest. All that he insisted upon was
this, that in imperial adventure the con-

quering race must abide by a moral code. A lie was a lie whether its victim be black or white. The European must respect the powers and rights of the Hindu as he would be compelled by law to respect them in his own State. "If we are not able," he said, "to contrive some method of governing India well which will not of necessity become the means of governing Great Britain ill, a ground is laid for their eternal separation, but none for sacrificing the people of that country to our constitution." England must be in India for India's benefit or not at all; political power and commercial monopoly such as the East India Company enjoyed could be had only insofar as they are instruments of right and not of violence. The Company's system was the antithesis of this. "There is nothing," he said in a magnificent passage, "before the eyes of the natives but an endless, hopeless prospect of new flights of birds of prey and passage, with appetites continually renewing for a food that is continually wasting." Sympathy with the native, regard for his habits and wants, the Company's servants failed to display. "The English youth in

India drink the intoxicating draught of
authority and dominion before their heads
are able to bear it, and as they are full
grown in fortune long before they are ripe
in principle, neither nature nor reason
have any opportunity to exert themselves
for the excesses of their premature power.
The consequences of their conduct, which
in good minds (and many of theirs are
probably such) might produce peni-
tence or amendment, are unable to
pursue the rapidity of their flight.
Their prey is lodged in England; and the
cries of India are given to seas and winds
to be blown about in every breaking up of
the monsoon over a remote and unhearing
ocean." More than a century was to pass
before the wisest of Burke's interpreters
attempted the translation of his maxims
into statute. But there has never, in any
language, been drawn a clearer picture of
the danger implicit in imperial adventure.
"The situation of man," said Burke, "is
the preceptor of his duty." He saw how
a nation might become corrupted by the
spoils of other lands. He knew that
cruelty abroad is the parent of a later
cruelty at home. Men will complain of

their wrongdoing in the remoter empire; and imperialism will employ the means Burke painted in unforgettable terms in his picture of Paul Benfield. He denied that the government of subject races can be regarded as a commercial transaction. Its problem was not to secure dividends but to accomplish moral benefit. He abhorred the politics of prestige. He knew the difficulties involved in administering distant territories, the ignorance and apathy of the public, the consequent erosion of responsibility, the chance that wrong will fail of discovery. But he did not shrink from his conclusion. "Let us do what we please," he said, "to put India from our thoughts, we can do nothing to separate it from our public interest and our national reputation." That is a general truth not less in Africa and China than in India itself. The main thought in Burke's mind was the danger lest colonial dominion become the breeding-ground of arbitrary ideas. That his own safeguards were inadequate is clear enough at the present time. He knew that the need was good government. He did not nor could he realize how intimately that ideal was connected with self-government. Yet the latest lesson is no more than the final outcome of his teaching.

IV

A background so consistent as this in the inflexible determination to moralize political action resulted in a noble edifice. Yet, through it all, the principles of policy are rather implied than admitted. It was when he came to deal with domestic problems and the French Revolution that Burke most clearly showed the real trend of his thought. That trend is unmistakable. Burke was a utilitarian who was convinced that what was old was valuable by the mere fact of its arrival at maturity. The State appeared to him an organic compound that came but slowly to its full splendour. It was easy to destroy; creation was impossible. Political philosophy was nothing for him but accurate generalization from experience; and he held the presumption to be against novelty. While he did not belittle the value of reason, he was always impressed by the immense part played by prejudice in the determi-

nation of policy. He had no doubt that
property was a rightful index to power;
and to disturb prescription seemed to him
the opening of the flood gates. Nor must
we miss the religious aspect of his philosophy. He never doubted that religion
was the foundation of the English State.
"Englishmen," he said in the *Reflections
on the French Revolution* (1790), "know,
and what is better, we feel inwardly, that
religion is the basis of civil society and the
source of all good and of all comfort."
The utterance is characteristic, not merely
in its depreciation of reason, but in its
ultimate reliance upon a mystic explanation of social facts. Nothing was more
alien from Burke's temper than deductive
thinking in politics. The only safeguard
he could find was in empiricism.

This hatred of abstraction is, of course,
the basis of his earliest publication; but it
remained with him to the end. He would
not discuss America in terms of right. "I
do not enter into these metaphysical distinctions," he said in the *Speech on
American Taxation*, "I hate the very
sound of them." "One sure symptom of
an ill-conducted state," he wrote in the

Reflections, "is the propensity of the people to resort to theories." "It is always to be lamented," he said in a *Speech on the Duration of Parliament,* "when men are driven to search into the foundations of the commonwealth." The theory of a social contract he declared "at best a confusion of judicial with civil principles," and he found no sense in the doctrine of popular sovereignty. "The lines of morality," he said in the *Appeal from the New to the Old Whigs* (1791), "are not like ideal lines of mathematics. They are broad and deep as well as long. They admit of exceptions; they demand modifications. These exceptions and modifications are made, not by the process of logic but by the rules of prudence. Prudence is not only first in rank of the virtues political and moral, but she is the director, the regulator, the standard of them all." Nor did he hesitate to draw the obvious conclusion. "This," he said, "is the true touchstone of all theories which regard man and the affairs of men — does it suit his nature in general, does it suit his nature as modified by his habits?"

Of the truth of this general attitude it is difficult to make denial. But when Burke came to apply it to the British Constitution the "rules of prudence" he was willing to admit are narrow enough to cause surprised enquiry. He did not doubt that the true end of a legislature was "to give a direction, a form, a technical dress . . . to the general sense of the community"; he admitted that popular revolt is so much the outcome of suffering that in any dispute between government and people, the presumption is at least equal in the latter's favor. He urged the acceptance of Grenville's bill for improving the method of decision upon disputed elections. He made a magnificent defence of the popular cause in the Middlesex election. He was in favor of the publication of parliamentary debates and of the voting lists in divisions. He supported almost with passion the ending of that iniquitous system by which the enfranchisement of revenue officers gave government a corrupt reservoir of electoral support. His *Speech on Economical Reform* (1780) was the prelude to a nobly-planned and successful attack upon the waste of the Civil list.

Yet beyond these measures Burke could never be persuaded to go. He was against the demand for shorter Parliaments on the excellent ground that the elections would be more corrupt and the Commons less responsible. He opposed the remedy of a Place Bill for the good and sufficient reason that it gave the executive an interest against the legislature. He would not, as in the great speech at Bristol (1774), accept the doctrine that a member of Parliament was a mere delegate of his constituents rather than a representative of his own convictions. "Government and legislation," he said, "are matters of reason and of judgment"; and once the private member had honorably arrived at a decision which he thought was for the interest of the whole community, his duty was done. All this, in itself, is unexceptionable; and it shows Burke's admirable grasp of the practical application of attractive theories to the event. But it is to be read in conjunction with a general hostility to basic constitutional change which is more dubious. He had no sympathy with the Radicals. "The bane of the Whigs," he said, "has been the admission

among them of the corps of schemers
. . . who do us infinite mischief by per-
suading many sober and well-meaning
people that we have designs inconsistent
with the Constitution left us by our fore-
fathers." "If the nation at large," he
wrote in another letter, "has disposition
enough to oppose all bad principles and
all bad men, its form of government is, in
my opinion, fully sufficient for it; but if
the general disposition be against a vir-
tuous and manly line of public conduct,
there is no form into which it can be
thrown that will improve its nature or add
to its energy"; and in the same letter he
foreshadows a possible retirement from
the House of Commons as a protest
against the growth of radical opinion in
his party. He resisted every effort to
reduce the suffrage qualification. He
had no sympathy with the effort either to
add to the county representation or to
abolish the rotten boroughs. The frame-
work of the parliamentary system seemed
to him excellent. He deplored all criticism of Parliament, and even the discussion of its essentials. "Our representation," he said, "is as nearly perfect as the

necessary imperfections of human affairs
and of human creatures will suffer it to
be." It was in the same temper that he
resisted all effort at the political relief of
the Protestant dissenters. "The machine
itself," he had said, "is well enough to
answer any good purpose, provided the
materials were sound"; and he never
moved from that opinion.

Burke's attitude was obsolete even
while he wrote; yet the suggestiveness of
his very errors makes examination of their
ground important. Broadly, he was protesting against natural right in the name
of expediency. His opponents argued
that, since men are by nature equal, it
must follow that they have an equal right
to self-government. To Burke, the admission of this principle would have
meant the overthrow of the British constitution. Its implication was that every
institution not of immediate popular
origin should be destroyed. To secure
their ends, he thought, the radicals were
compelled to preach the injustice of those
institutions and thus to injure that affection for government upon which peace
and security depend. Here was an effort

to bring all institutions to the test of logic
which he thought highly dangerous. "No
rational man ever did govern himself," he
said, "by abstractions and universals."
The question for him was not the abstract
rightness of the system upon some set of
a priori principles but whether, on the
whole, that system worked for the happiness of the community. He did not doubt
that it did; and to overthrow a structure
so nobly tested by the pressure of events
in favor of some theories outside historic
experience seemed to him ruinous to society. Government, for him, was the general harmony of diverse interests; and the
continual adjustments and exquisite
modifications of which it stood in need
were admirably discovered in the existing
system. Principles were thus unimportant compared to the problem of their application. "The major," he said of all
political premises, "makes a pompous
figure in the battle, but the victory depends upon the little minor of circumstances."

To abstract natural right he therefore
opposed prescription. The presumption
of wisdom is on the side of the past, and

when we change, we act at our peril.
"Prescription," he said in 1782, "is the
most solid of all titles, not only to property, but to what is to secure that property, to government." Because he saw
the State organically he was impressed by
the smallness both of the present moment
and the individual's thought. It is built
upon the wisdom of the past for "the
species is wise, and when time is given to
it, as a species it almost always acts right."
And since it is the past alone which has
had the opportunity to accumulate this
rightness our disposition should be to preserve all ancient things. They could not
be without a reason; and that reason is
grounded upon ancestral experience. So
the prescriptive title becomes "not the
creature, but the master, of positive law
. . . the soundest, the most general and
the most recognized title between man and
man that is known in municipal or public
jurisprudence." It is by prescription that
he defends the existence of Catholicism in
Ireland not less than the supposed deformities of the British Constitution. So,
too, his main attack on atheism is its implication that "everything is to be dis-

cussed." He does not say that all which
is has rightness in it; but at least he urges
that to doubt it is to doubt the construction
of a past experience which built according
to the general need. Nor does he doubt
the chance that what he urges may be
wrong. Rather does he insist that at least
it gives us security, for him the highest
good. "Truth," he said, "may be far
better . . . but as we have scarcely ever
that certainty in the one that we have in
the other, I would, unless the truth were
evident indeed, hold fast to peace, which
has in her company charity, the highest of
the virtues."

Such a philosophy, indeed, so barely
stated, would seem a defence of political
immobility; but Burke attempted safeguards against that danger. His insistence upon the superior value of past experience was balanced by a general admission that particular circumstances
must always govern the immediate decision. "When the reason of old establishments is gone," he said in his *Speech
on Economical Reform,* "it is absurd to
preserve nothing but the burden of them."
"A disposition to preserve and an ability

to improve," he wrote in the *Reflections on the French Revolution,* "taken together would be my standard of a statesman." But that "ability to improve" conceals two principles of which Burke never relaxed his hold. "All the reformations we have hitherto made," he said, "have proceeded upon the principle of reference to antiquity"; and the *Appeal from the New to the Old Whigs,* which is the most elaborate exposition of his general attitude, proceeds upon the general basis that 1688 is a perpetual model for the future. Nor is this all. "If I cannot reform with equity," said Burke, "I will not reform at all"; and equity seems here to mean a sacrifice of the present and its passionate demands to the selfish errors of past policy.

Burke, indeed, was never a democrat, and that is the real root of his philosophy. He saw the value of the party-system, and he admitted the necessity of some degree of popular representation. But he was entirely satisfied with current Whig principles, could they but be purged of their grosser deformities. He knew too well how little reason is wont to enter into the

formation of political opinion to make the
sacrifice of innovation to its power. He
saw so much of virtue in the old order,
that he insisted upon the equation of
virtue with quintessence. Men of great
property and position using their influence as a public trust, delicate in their
sense of honor, and acting only from motives of right — these seemed to him the
men who should with justice exercise political power. He did not doubt that
"there is no qualification for government
but virtue and wisdom . . . wherever
they are actually found, they have, in
whatever state, condition, profession or
trade, the passport to heaven"; but he is
careful to dissociate the possibility that
they can be found in those who practice
the mechanical arts. He did not mean
that his aristocracy should govern without
response to popular demand. He had no
objection to criticism, nor to the public
exercise of government. There was no
reason even for agreement, so long as each
party was guided by an honorable sense of
the public good. This, so he urged, was
the system which underlay the temporary
evils of the British Constitution. An aris-

tocracy delegated to do its work by the mass of men was the best form of government his imagination could conceive. It meant that property must be dominant in the system of government, that, while office should be open to all, it should be out of the reach of most. "The characteristic essence of property," he wrote in the *Reflections,* ". . . is to be unequal"; and he thought the perpetuation of that inequality by inheritance "that which tends most to the perpetuation of society itself." The system was difficult to maintain, and it must be put out of the reach of popular temptation. "Our constitution," he said in the *Present Discontents,* "stands on a nice equipoise, with sharp precipices and deep waters on all sides of it. In removing it from a dangerous leaning towards one side, there may be a danger towards oversething it on the other." In straining, that is to say, after too large a purification, we may end with destruction. And Burke, of course, was emphatic upon the need that property should be undisturbed. It was always, he thought, at a great disadvantage in any struggle with ability; and there are many

passages in which he urges the consequent
special representation which the adequate
defence of property requires.

The argument, at bottom, is common to
all thinkers over-impressed by the sanctity
of past experience. Hegel and Savigny
in Germany, Taine and Renan in France,
Sir Henry Maine and Lecky in England,
have all urged what is in effect a similar
plea. We must not break what Bagehot
called the cake of custom, for men have
been trained to its digestion, and new food
breeds trouble. Laws are the offspring of
the original genius of a people, and while
we may renovate, we must not unduly reform. The true idea of national development is always latent in the past
experience of the race and it is from that
perpetual spring alone that wisdom can
be drawn. We render obedience to what
is with effortless unconsciousness; and
without this loyalty to inherited institutions the fabric of society would be dissolved. Civilization, in fact, depends upon
the performance of actions defined in pre-
conceived channels; and if we obeyed
those novel impulses of right which seem,
at times, to contradict our inheritance, we

should disturb beyond repair the intricate
equilibrium of countless ages. The experience of the past rather than the desires
of the present is thus the true guide to
our policy. "We ought," he said in a
famous sentence, "to venerate where we
are unable presently to comprehend."

It is easy to see why a mind so attuned
recoiled from horror at the French Revolution. There is something almost sinister
in the destiny which confronted Burke
with the one great spectacle of the eighteenth century which he was certain not
merely to misunderstand but also to hate.
He could not endure the most fragmen-
tary change in tests of religious belief;
and the Revolution swept overboard the
whole religious edifice. He would not
support the abolition even of the most
flagrant abuses in the system of representation; and he was to see in France an
overthrow of a monarchy even more
august in its prescriptive rights than the
English Parliament. Privileges were
scattered to the winds in a single night.
Peace was sacrificed to exactly those
metaphysical theories of equality and justice which he most deeply abhorred. The

doctrine of progress found an eloquent
defender in that last and noblest utterance
of Condorcet which is still perhaps its
most perfect justification. On all hands
there was the sense of a new world built
by the immediate thought of man upon
the wholehearted rejection of past history.
Politics was emphatically declared to be
a system of which the truths could be
stated in terms of mathematical certainty.
The religious spirit which Burke was convinced lay at the root of good gave way
before a general scepticism which, from
the outset of his life, he had declared incompatible with social order. Justice was
asserted to be the centre of social right;
and it was defined as the overthrow of
those prescriptive privileges which Burke
regarded as the protective armour of the
body politic. Above all, the men who
seized the reins of power became convinced that theirs was a specific of universal application. Their disciples in
England seemed in the same diabolic
frenzy with themselves. In a moment of
time, the England which had been the example to Europe of ordered popular liberty became, for these enthusiasts, only

less barbaric than the despotic princes of
the continent. That Price and Priestley
should suffer the infection was, even for
Burke, a not unnatural thing. But when
Charles Fox cast aside the teaching of
twenty years for its antithesis, Burke
must have felt that no price was too great
to pay for the overthrow of the Revolution.

Certainly his pamphlets on events in
France are at every point consistent with
his earlier doctrine. The charge that he
supported the Revolution in America and
deserted it in France is without meaning;
for in the one there is no word that can
honorably be twisted to support the other.
And when we make allowances for the
grave errors of personal taste, the gross
exaggeration, the inability to see the
Revolution as something more than a
single point in time, it becomes obvious
enough that his criticism, de Maistre's
apart, is by far the soundest we possess
from the generation which knew the movement as a living thing. The attempt to
produce an artificial equality upon which
he seized as the essence of the Revolution
was, as Mirabeau was urging in private

to the king, the inevitable precursor of dictatorship. He realized that freedom is born of a certain spontaneity for which the rigid lines of doctrinaire thinkers left no room. That worship of symmetrical form which underlies the constitutional experiments of the next few years he exposed in a sentence which has in it the essence of political wisdom. "The nature of man is intricate"; he wrote in the *Reflections,* "the objects of society are of the greatest possible complexity; and therefore no simple disposition or direction of power can be suitable either to man's nature or to the quality of his affairs." The note recurs in substance throughout his criticism. Much of its application, indeed, will not stand for one moment the test of inquiry; as when, for instance, he correlates the monarchical government of France with the English constitutional system and extols the perpetual virtues of 1688. The French made every effort to find the secret of English principles, but the roots were absent from their national experience.

A year after the publication of the *Reflections* he himself perceived the narrowness of that judgment. In the *Thoughts on French Affairs* (1791) he saw that the essence of the Revolution was its foundation in theoretic dogma. It was like nothing else in the history of the world except the Reformation; which last event it especially resembles in its genius for self-propagation. Herein he has already envisaged the importance of that *"patrie intellectuelle"* which Tocqueville emphasized as born of the Revolution. That led Burke once again to insist upon the peculiar genius of each separate state, the difficulties of a change, the danger of grafting novelties upon an ancient fabric. He saw the certainty that in adhering to an abstract metaphysical scheme the French were in truth omitting human nature from their political equation; for general ideas can find embodiment in institutional forms only after they have been moulded by a thousand varieties of circumstance. The French created an universal man not less destructive of their practical sagacity than the Frankenstein of the economists. They omitted, as Burke saw, the elements which objective experience must demand; with the result

that, despite themselves, they came rather
to destroy than to fulfil. Napoleon, as
Burke prophesied, reaped the harvest of
their failure.

Nor was he less right in his denuncia-
tion of that distrust of the past which
played so large a part in the revolutionary consciousness. "We are afraid," he
wrote in the *Reflections,* "to put men to
live and trade each on his own private
stock of reason, because we suspect that
this stock in each man is small, and that
the individuals would do better to avail
themselves of the general bank and capital of nations and of ages." Of Siéyès'
building constitutions overnight, this is no
unfair picture; but it points a more general truth never long absent from Burke's
mind. Man is for him so much the creature of prejudice, so much a mosaic of
ancestral tradition, that the chance of
novel thought finding a peaceful place
among his institutions is always small.
For Burke, thought is always at the
service of the instincts, and these lie buried
in the remote experience of the state. So
that men like Robespierre were asking
from their subjects an impossible task.

That which they had conceived in the gray abstractness of their speculations was too little related to what the average Frenchman knew and desired to be enduring. Burke looks with sober admiration at the way in which the English revolution related itself at every point to ideas and theories with which the average man was as familiar as with the physical landmarks of his own neighborhood. For the motives which underlie all human effort are, he thought, sufficiently constant to compel regard. That upon which they feed submits to change; but the effort is slow and the disappointments many. The Revolution taught the populace the thirst for power. But it failed to remember that sense of continuity in human effort without which new constructions are built on sand. The power it exercised lacked that horizon of the past through which alone it suffers limitation to right ends.

The later part of Burke's attack upon the Revolution does not belong to political philosophy. No man is more responsible than he for the temper which drew England into war. He came to write rather with the zeal of a fanatic waging a holy

war than in the temper of a statesman
confronted with new ideas. Yet even the
Letters on a Regicide Peace (1796) have
flashes of the old, incomparable insight;
and they show that even in the midst of
his excesses he did not war for love of it.
So that it is permissible to think he did
not lightly pen those sentences on peace
which stand as oases of wisdom in a desert
of extravagant rhetoric. "War never
leaves where it found a nation," he wrote,
"it is never to be entered upon without
mature deliberation." That was a lesson
his generation had still to learn; nor did
it take to heart the even nobler passage
that follows. "The blood of man," he
said, "should never be shed but to redeem
the blood of man. It is well shed for our
family, for our friends, for our God, for
our country, for mankind. The rest is
vanity; the rest is crime." It is perhaps
the most tragic wrong in that century's
history that these words were written to
justify an effort of which they supply an
irrefutable condemnation.

V

Criticism of Burke's theories can be made from at least two angles. It is easy to show that his picture of the British Constitution was remote from the facts even when he wrote. Every change that he opposed was essential to the security of the next generation; and there followed none of the disastrous consequences he had foreshadowed. Such criticism would be at almost every point just; and yet it would fail to touch the heart of Burke's position. What is mainly needed is analysis at once of his omissions and of the underlying assumptions of what he wrote. Burke came to his maturity upon the eve of the Industrial Revolution; and we have it upon the authority of Adam Smith himself that no one had so clearly apprehended his own economic principles. Yet there is no word in what Burke had to say of their significance. The vast agrarian changes of the time contained, as it appears, no special moment even for him who burdened himself unduly to restore the Beaconsfield estate. No man was more eager than he that the public should be admitted to the

mysteries of political debate; yet he stead-
fastly refused to draw the obvious infer-
ence that once the means of government
were made known those who possessed the
knowledge would demand their share in
its application. He did not see that the
metaphysics he so profoundly distrusted
was itself the offspring of that contemptible worship of expediency which Blackstone generalized into a legalistic jargon.
Men never move to the adumbration of
general right until the conquest of political rights has been proved inadequate.
That Burke himself may be said in a sense
to have seen when he insisted upon the
danger of examining the foundations of
the State. Yet a man who refuses to admit that the constant dissatisfaction with
those foundations his age expressed is the
expression of serious ill in the body politic
is wilfully blind to the facts at issue. No
one had more faithfully than Burke himself explained why the Whig oligarchy
was obsolete; yet nothing would induce him
ever to realize that the alternative to aristocratic government is democracy and
that its absence was the cause of that dis-
quiet of which he realized that Wilkes was
but the symptom.

Broadly, that is to say, Burke would not realize that the reign of political privilege was drawing to its close. That is the real meaning of the French Revolution and therein it represents a stream of tendency not less active in England than abroad. In France, indeed, the lines were more sharply drawn than elsewhere. The rights men craved were not, as Burke insisted, the immediate offspring of metaphysic fancy, but the result of a determination to end the malignant wrong of centuries. A power that knew no responsibility, war and intolerance that derived only from the accidental caprice of the court, arrest that bore no relation to offence, taxation inversely proportionate to the ability to pay, these were the prescriptive privileges that Burke invited his generation to accept as part of the accumulated wisdom of the past. It is not difficult to see why those who swore their oath in the tennis-court at Versailles should have felt such wisdom worthy to be condemned. Burke's caution was for them the timidity of one who embraces existent evils rather than fly to the refuge of an accessible good. In a less degree, the same is true of England. The constitution that Burke called upon men to worship was the constitution which made the Duke of Bedford powerful, that gave no representation to Manchester and a member to Old Sarum, which enacted the game laws and left upon the statute-book a penal code which hardly yielded to the noble attack of Romilly. These, which were for Burke merely the accidental excrescences of a noble ideal, were for them its inner essence; and where they could not reform they were willing to destroy.

The revolutionary spirit, in fact, was as much the product of the past as the very institutions it came to condemn. The innovations were the inevitable outcome of past oppression. Burke refused to see that aspect of the picture. He ascribed to the crime of the present what was due to the half-wilful errors of the past. The man who grounded his faith in historic experience refused to admit as history the elements alien from his special outlook. He took that liberty not to venerate where he was unable to comprehend which he denied to his opponents. Nor did he admit the uses to which his doctrine of pre-

scription was bound to be put in the hands
of selfish and unscrupulous men. No one
will object to privilege for a Chatham;
but privilege for the Duke of Grafton is a
different thing, and Burke's doctrine safeguards the innumerable men of whom
Grafton is the type in the hope that by
happy accident some Chatham will one
day emerge. He justifies the privileges
of the English Church in the name of religious well-being; but it is difficult to see
what men like Watson or Archbishop
Cornwallis have got to do with religion.
The doctrine of prescription might be admirable if all statesmen were so wise as
Burke; but in the hands of lesser men it
becomes no more than the protective armour of vested interests into the ethics of
which it refuses us leave to examine.

That suspicion of thought is integral to
Burke's philosophy, and it deserves more
examination than it has received. In part
it is a rejection of the Benthamite position
that man is a reasoning animal. It puts
its trust in habit as the chief source of
human action; and it thus is distrustful of
thought as leading into channels to which
the nature of man is not adapted. Nov-

elty, which is assumed to be the outcome
of thought, it regards as subversive of the
routine upon which civilization depends.
Thought is destructive of peace; and it is
argued that we know too little of political
phenomena to make us venture into the
untried places to which thought invites us.
Yet the first of many answers is surely
the most obvious fact that if man is so
much the creature of his custom no reason
would prevail save where they proved inadequate. If thought is simply a reserve
power in society, its strength must obviously depend upon common acceptance;
and that can only come when some routine
has failed to satisfy the impulses of men.

But we may urge a difficulty that is even
more decisive. No system of habits can
ever hope to endure long in a world where
the cumulative power of memory enables
change to be so swift; and no system of
habits can endure at all unless its underlying idea represents the satisfaction of a
general desire. It must, that is to say,
make rational appeal; and, indeed, as
Aristotle said, it can have virtue only to
the point where it is conscious of itself.
The uncritical routine of which Burke is

the sponsor would here deprive the mass of men of virtue. Yet in modern civilization the whole strength of any custom depends upon exactly that consciousness of right which Burke restricted to his aristocracy. Our real need is less the automatic response to ancient stimulus than power to know what stimulus has social value. We need, that is to say, the gift of criticism rather than the gift of inert acceptance. Not, of course, that the habits which Burke so earnestly admired are at all part of our nervous endowment in any integral sense. The short space of the French Revolution made the habit of thinking in terms of progress an essential part of our intellectual inheritance; and where the Burkian school proclaims how exceptional progress has been in history, we take that as proof of the ease with which essential habit may be acquired. Habit, in fact, without philosophy destroys the finer side of civilized life. It may leave a stratum to whom its riches have been discovered; but it leaves the mass of men soulless automata without spontaneous response to the chords struck by another hand.

Burke's answer would, of course, have been that he was not a democrat. He did not trust the people and he rated their capacity as low. He thought of the people — it was obviously a generalization from his time — as consistently prone to disorder and checked only by the force of ancient habit. Yet he has himself supplied the answer to that attitude. "My observation," he said in his *Speech on the East India Bill,* "has furnished me with nothing that is to be found in any habits of life or education which tends wholly to disqualify men for the functions of government." We can go further than that sober caution. We know that there is one technique only capable of securing good government and that is the training of the mass of men to interest in it. We know that no State can hope for peace in which large types of experience are without representation. Indeed, if proof were here wanting, an examination of the eighteenth century would supply it. Few would deny that statesmen are capable of disinterested sacrifice for classes of whose inner life they are ignorant; yet the relation between law and the interest of the dominant class is too intimate to permit with safety the exclusion of a part of the State from sharing in its guidance. Nor did Burke remember his own wise saying that "in all disputes between the people and their rulers the presumption is at least upon a par in favor of the people"; and he quotes with agreement that great sentence of Sully's which traces popular violence to popular suffering. No one can watch the economic struggles of the eighteenth and nineteenth centuries or calculate the pain they have involved to humble men, without admitting that they represent the final protest of an outraged mind against oppression too intolerable to be borne. Burke himself, as his own speeches show, knew little or nothing of the pain involved in the agrarian changes of his age. The one way to avoid violent outbreak is not exclusion of the people from power but their participation in it. The popular sense of right may often, as Aristotle saw, be wiser than the opinion of statesmen. It is not necessary to equate the worth of untrained commonsense with experienced wisdom to suggest that, in the long run, neglect of common sense will make the effort of that wisdom fruitless.

This, indeed, is to take the lowest
ground. For the case against Burke's
aristocracy has a moral aspect with which
he did not deal. He did not inquire by
what right a handful of men were to be
hereditary governors of a whole people.
Expediency is no answer to the question,
for Bentham was presently to show how
shallow was that basis of consent. Once
it is admitted that the personality of men
is entitled to respect institutional room
must be found for its expression. The
State is morally stunted where their
powers go undeveloped. There is something curious here in Burke's inability to
suspect deformity in a system which gave
his talents but partial place. He must
have known that no one in the House of
Commons was his equal. He must have
known how few of those he called upon to
recognize the splendor of their function
were capable of playing the part he pic-
tured for them. The answer to a morally
bankrupt aristocracy is surely not the
overwhelming effort required in its purification when the plaintiff is the people;
for the mere fact that the people is the
plaintiff is already evidence of its fitness

for power. Burke gave no hint of how
the level of his governing class could be
maintained. He said nothing of what education might accomplish for the people.
He did not examine the obvious consequences of their economic status. Had
his eyes not been obscured by passion the
work of that States-General the names in
which appeared to him so astonishing in
their inexperience, might have given him
pause. The "obscure provincial advo-
cates . . . stewards of petty local ju-
risdictions . . . the fomenters and
conductors of the petty war of village vex-
ation" legislated, out of their inexperience,
for the world. Their resolution, their
constancy, their high sense of the national
need, were precisely the qualities Burke
demanded in his governing class; and the
States-General did not move from the
straight path he laid down until they met
with intrigue from those of whom Burke
became the licensed champion.

Nor is it in the least clear that his emphasis upon expediency is, in any real
way, a release from metaphysical inquiry.
Rather may it be urged that what was
needed in Burke's philosophy was the

clear avowal of the metaphysic it implied.
Nothing is more greatly wanted in political inquiry than discovery of that "intu-
ition more subtle than any articulate
major premise" which, as Mr. Justice
Holmes has said, is the true foundation of
so many of our political judgments. The
theory of natural rights upon which
Burke heaped such contempt was wrong
rather in its form than in its substance. It
clearly suffered from its mistaken effort
to trace to an imaginary state of nature
what was due to a complex experience.
It suffered also from its desire to lay down
universal formulæ. It needed to state the
rights demanded in terms of the social interests they involved rather than in the
abstract ethic they implied. But the demands which underlay the thought of men
like Price and Priestley was as much the
offspring of experience as Burke's own
doctrine. They made, indeed, the tactical
mistake of seeking to give an unripe philosophic form to a political strategy wherein, clearly enough, Burke was their
master. But no one can read the answers
of Paine and Mackintosh, who both were
careful to avoid the panoply of meta-

physics, to the *Reflections,* without feeling
that Burke failed to move them from their
main position. Expediency may be admirable in telling the statesmen what to
do; but it does not explain the sources of
his ultimate act, nor justify the thing
finally done. The unconscious deeps
which lie beneath the surface of the mind
are rarely less urgent than the motives
that are avowed. Action is less their elim-
ination than their index; and we must
penetrate within their recesses before we
have the full materials for judgment.

Considered in this fashion, the case for
natural rights is surely unanswerable.
The things that men desire correspond, in
some rough fashion, to the things they
need. Natural rights are nothing more
than the armour evolved to protect their
vital interests. Upon the narrow basis of
legal history it is, of course, impossible to
protect them. History is rather the record
of the thwarting of human desire than of
its achievement. But upon the value of
certain things there is a sufficient and constant opinion to give us assurance that
repression will ultimately involve disorder.
Nor is there any difference between the

classes of men in this regard. Forms, indeed, will vary; and the power we have of answering demand will always wait upon the discoveries of science. Our natural rights, that is to say, will have a changing content simply because this is not a static world. But that does not mean, as Burke insisted, that they are empty of experience. They come, of course, mainly from men who have been excluded from intimate contact with the fruits of power. Nonconformists in religion, workers without land or capital save the power of their own hands, it is from the disinherited that they draw, as demands, their strength. Yet it is difficult to see, as Burke would undoubtedly have insisted, that they are the worse from the source whence they derive. Rather do they point to grave inadequacy in the substance of the state, inadequacy neglect of which has led to the cataclysms of historic experience. The unwillingness of Burke to examine into their foundation reveals his lack of moral insight into the problem he confronted.

That lack of insight must, of course, be given some explanation; and its cause seems rooted in Burke's metaphysic outlook. He was profoundly religious; and he did not doubt that the order of the universe was the command of God. It was, as a consequence, beneficent; and to deny its validity was, for him, to doubt the wisdom of God. "Having disposed," he wrote, "and marshalled us by a divine tactic, not according to our will, but to His, He had, in and by that disposition, vitally subjected us to act the part which belongs to the place assigned us." The State, in fact, it is to be built upon the sacrifice of men; and this they must accept as of the will of God. We are to do our duty in our allotted station without repining, in anticipation, doubtless, of a later reward. What we are is thus the expression of his goodness; and there is a real sense in which Burke may be said to have maintained the inherent rightness of the existing order. Certainly he throws a cloak of religious veneration about the purely metaphysical concept of property; and his insistence upon the value of peace as opposed to truth is surely part of the same attitude. Nor is it erroneous to connect this background with his antagonism to the French Revolution. What there was

most distressing to him was the over-
throwal of the Church, and he did not hesitate, in very striking fashion, to connect
revolutionary opinion with infidelity. Indeed Burke, like Locke, seems to have
been convinced that a social sense was impossible in an atheist; and his *Letters on
a Regicide Peace* have a good deal of that
relentless illogic which made de Maistre
connect the first sign of dissent from ul-
tramontanism with the road to a denial of
all faith. Nothing is more difficult than
to deal with a thinker who has had a reve-
lation; and this sense that the universe was
a divine mystery not to be too nearly
scrutinized by man grew greatly upon
Burke in his later years. It was not an
attitude which reason could overthrow;
for its first principle was an awe in the
presence of facts to which reason is a
stranger.

There is, moreover, in Burke a Platonic
idealism which made him, like later
thinkers of the school, regard existing
difficulties with something akin to complacent benevolence. What interested
him was the idea of the English State;
and whatever, as he thought, deformed it,

was not of the essence of its nature. He
denied, that is to say, that the degree to
which a purpose is fulfilled is as important
as the purpose itself. A thing becomes
good by the end it has in view; and the
deformities of time and place ought not
to lead us to deny the beauty of the end.
It is the great defect of all idealistic philosophy that it should come to the examination of facts in so optimistic a temper.
It never sufficiently realizes that in the
transition from theoretic purpose to practical realization a significant transforma-
tion may occur. We do not come to grips
with the facts. What we are bidden to
remember is the splendor of what the facts
are trying to be. The existing order is
beatified as a necessary stage in a beneficent process. We are not to separate
out the constituent elements therein, and
judge them as facts in time and space.
Society is one and indivisible; and the defects do not at any point impair the ultimate integrity of the social bond.

Yet it is surely evident that in the heat
and stress of social life, we cannot afford
so long a period as the basis for our judgment. We may well enough regard the

corruption of the monarchy under the later Hanoverians as the neçessary prelude to its purification under Victoria; but that does not make it any the less corrupt. We may even see how a monistic view of society is possible to one who, like Burke, is uniquely occupied with the public good. But the men who, like Muir and Hardy in the treason trials of the Revolution, think rather in terms of the existing disharmonies than the beauty of the purpose upon which they rest, are only human if they think those disharmonies more real than the purpose they do not meet. They were surely to be pardoned if, reading the *Reflections* of Burke, they regarded class distinctions as more vital than their harmony of interest, when they saw the tenacity with which privileges they did not share were defended. It is even possible to understand why some insisted that if those privileges were, as Burke had argued, essential to the construction of the whole, it was against that whole, alike in purpose and in realization, that they were in revolt. For them the fact of discontinuity was vital. They could not but ask for happiness in their own individual lives no less than in the State of which they were part. They came to see that without self-government in the sense of their own active participation in power, such happiness must go unfulfilled. The State, in fact, may have the noblest purpose; but its object is attempted by agents who are also mortal men. The basis of their scrutiny became at once pragmatic. The test of allegiance to established institutions became immediately the achievement for which they were responsible. The achievement, as they urged, was hardly written with adequacy in terms of the lives of humble men. That was why they judged no attitude of worth which sought the equation of the real and the ideal. The first lesson of their own experience of power was the need for its limitation by the instructed judgment of free minds.[1]

VI

No man was more deeply hostile to the early politics of the romantic movement. to the *Contrat Social* of Rousseau and the *Political Justice* of Godwin, than was

[1] Cf. my *Authority in the Modern State*, pp. 65-9.

Burke; yet, on the whole, it is with the romantics that Burke's fundamental influence remains. His attitude to reason, his exaltation of passion and imagination over the conscious logic of men, were of the inmost stuff of which they were made. In that sense, at least, his kinship is with the great conservative revolution of the generation which followed him. Hegel and Savigny in Germany, de Maistre and Bonald in France, Coleridge and the later Wordsworth in England, are in a true sense his disciples. That does not mean that any of them were directly conscious of his work but that the movement he directed had its necessary outcome in their defence of his ideals. The path of history is strewn with undistributed middles; and it is possible that in the clash between his attitude and that of Bentham there were the materials for a fuller synthesis in a later time. Certainly there is no more admirable corrective in historical politics that the contrast they afford.

It is easy to praise Burke and easier still to miss the greatness of his effort. Perspective apart, he is destined doubtless to live rather as the author of some

maxims that few statesmen will dare to
forget than as the creator of a system
which, even in its unfinished implications,
is hardly less gigantic than that of Hobbes
or Bentham. His very defects are lessons
in themselves. His unhesitating inability
to see how dangerous is the concentration
of property is standing proof that men are
over-prone to judge the rightness of a
State by their own wishes. His own contempt for the results of reasonable inquiry
is a ceaseless lesson in the virtue of consistent scrutiny of our inheritance. His
disregard of popular desire suggests the
fatal ease with which we neglect the
opinion of those who stand outside the
active centre of political conflict. Above
all, his hostility to the Revolution should
at least make later generations beware lest
novelty of outlook be unduly confounded
with erroneous doctrine.

Yet even when such deduction has been
made, there is hardly a greater figure in
the history of political thought in England. Without the relentless logic of
Hobbes, the acuteness of Hume, the
moral insight of T. H. Green, he has a
large part of the faculties of each. He

brought to the political philosophy of his
generation a sense of its direction, a lofty
vigour of purpose, and a full knowledge
of its complexity, such as no other statesman has ever possessed. His flashes of
insight are things that go, as few men have
ever gone, into the hidden deeps of political complexity. Unquestionably, his
speculation is rather that of the orator in
the tribune than of the thinker in his
study. He never forgot his party, and he
wrote always in that House of Commons
atmosphere which makes a man unjust to
the argument and motives of his opponent. Yet, when the last word of criticism has been made, the balance of
illumination is immense. He illustrates
at its best the value of that party-system
the worth of which made so deep an impression on all he wrote. He showed that
government by discussion can be made to
illuminate great principles. He showed
also that allegiance to party is never inconsistent with the deeper allegiance to
the demand of conscience. When he came
to the House of Commons, the prospects
of representative government were very
dark; and it is mainly to his emphasis

upon its virtues that its victory must be attributed. Institutional change is likely to be more rapid than in his generation; for we seem to have reached that moment when, as he foresaw, "they who persist in opposing that mighty current will appear rather to resist the decrees of Providence itself than the mere designs of men." The principles upon which we proceed are doubtless different from those that he commended; yet his very challenge to their wisdom only gives to his warning a deeper inspiration for our effort.

CHAPTER VII

THE FOUNDATIONS OF ECONOMIC
LIBERALISM

I

THE Industrial Revolution is hardly
less a fundamental change in the habits of
English thought than in the technique of
commercial production. Alongside the
discoveries of Hargreaves and Crompton,
the ideas of Hume and Adam Smith
shifted the whole perspective of men's
minds. The Revolution, indeed, like all
great movements, did not originate at any
given moment. There was no sudden in-
vention which made the hampering system
of government-control seem incompatible
with industrial advance. The mercantilism against which the work of Adam
Smith was so magistral a protest was
already rather a matter of external than
internal commerce when he wrote. He
triumphed less because he suddenly
opened men's eyes to a truth hitherto concealed than because he represented the

culmination of certain principles which,
under various aspects, were common to his
time.　The movement for religious toleration is not only paralleled in the next century by the movement for economic
freedom, but is itself in a real sense the
parent of the latter.　For it is not without
significance that the pre-Adamite economists were almost without exception the
urgent defenders of religious toleration.
The landowners were churchmen, the men
of commerce largely Nonconformist; and
religious proscription interfered with the
balance of trade.　When the roots of religious freedom had been secured, it was
easy for them to transfer their argument
to the secular sphere.

Nothing, indeed, is more important in
the history of English political philosophy
than to realize that from Stuart times the
Nonconformists were deeply bitten with
distrust of government.　Its courts of
special instance hampered industrial life
at every turn in the interest of religious
conformity.　Their heavy fines and irritating restrictions upon foreign workmen
were nothing so much as a tax upon industrial progress.　What the Nonconformists

wanted was to be left alone; and Davenant explained the root of their desire
when he tells of the gaols crowded with
substantial tradesmen whose imprison-
ment spelt unemployment for thousands
of workmen. Sir William Temple, in his
description of Holland, represents economic prosperity as the child of toleration.
The movement for ecclesiastical freedom
in England, moreover, became causally
linked with that protest against the system
of monopolies with which it was the habit
of the court to reward its favorites. Freedom in economic matters, like freedom in
religion, came rapidly to mean permission
that diversity shall exist; and economic
diversity soon came to mean free competition. The latter easily became imbued
with religious significance. English puritanism, as Troeltsch has shown us, insisted that work was the will of God and
its performance the test of grace. The
greater the energy of its performance, the
greater the likelihood of prosperity; and
thence it is but a step to argue that the
free development of a man's industrial
worth is the law of God. Success in business, indeed, became for many a test of

religious grace, and poverty the proof of
God's disfavor. Books like Steele's *Religious Tradesman* (1684) show clearly
how close is the connection. The hostility
of the English landowners to the commercial classes in the eighteenth century
is at bottom the inheritance of religious
antagonism. The typical qualities of dissent became a certain pushful exertion by
which the external criteria of salvation
could be secured.

Much of the contemporary philosophy,
moreover, fits in with this attitude. From
the time of Bacon, the main object of
speculation was to disrupt the scholastic
teleology. In the result the State becomes
dissolved into a discrete mass of individuals, and the self-interest of each is the
starting-point of all inquiry. Hobbes
built his state upon the selfishness of men;
even Locke makes the individual enter political life for the benefits that accrue
therefrom. The cynicism of Mandeville,
the utilitarianism of Hume, are only by-paths of the same tradition. The organic
society of the middle ages gives place to
an individual who builds the State out of
his own desires. Liberty becomes their

realization; and the object of the State is
to enable men in the fullest sense to secure
the satisfaction of their private wants.
How far is that conception from the Anglican outlook of the seventeenth century,
a sermon of Laud's makes clear. "If any
man," he said,[1] "be so addicted to his private interest that he neglects the common
State, he is void of the sense of piety, and
wishes peace and happiness for himself in
vain. For, whoever he be, he must live in
the body of the commonwealth and in the
body of the Church." So Platonic an outlook was utterly alien from the temper of
puritanism. They had no thought of sacrificing themselves to an institution which
they had much ground for thinking existed only for their torment. The development of the religious instinct to the level
of salvation found its philosophic ana-
logue in the development of the economic
sense of fitness. The State became the
servant of the individual from being his
master; and service became equated with
an internal policy of *laissez-faire*.

Such summary, indeed, abridges the

[1] Sermon of June 19, 1621. Works (ed. of 1847),
p. 28.

long process of release from which the eighteenth century had still to suffer; nor does it sufficiently insist upon the degree to which the old idea of state control still held sway in external policies of trade. Mercantilism was still in the ascendant when Adam Smith came to write. Few statesmen of importance before the younger Pitt had learned the secret of its fallacies; and, indeed, the chief ground for difference between Chatham and Burke was the former's suspicion that Burke had embraced the noxious doctrine of free trade. Mercantilism, by the time of Locke, is not the simple error that wealth consists in bullion but the insistence that the balance of trade must be preserved. Partly it was doubtless derived from the methods of the old political arithmetic of men like Petty and Davenant; the individual seeks a balance at the end of his year's accounting and so, too, the State must have a balance. "A Kingdom," said Locke, "grows rich or poor just as a farmer does, and no other way"; and while there is a sense in which this is wholly true, the meaning attached to it by the mercantilists was that foreign competition meant national weakness. They could not conceive a commercial bargain which was profitable to both sides. Nations grow prosperous at each other's expense; wherefore a woolen trade in Ireland necessarily spells English unemployment. Even Davenant, who was in many respects on the high road to free trade, was in this problem adamant. Protection was essential in the colonial market; for unless the trade of the colonies was directed through England they might be dangerous rivals. So Ireland and America were sacrificed to the fear of British merchants, with the inevitable result that repression brought from both the obvious search for remedy.

Herein it might appear that Adam Smith had novelty to contribute; yet nothing is more certain than that his full sense of the world as the only true unit of marketing was fully grasped before him. In 1691 Sir Dudley North published his *Discourses upon Trade*. Therein he clearly sees that commercial barriers between Great Britain and France are basically as senseless as would be commercial barriers between Yorkshire and Middlesex. Indeed, in one sense, North goes even further than Adam Smith, for he argues against the usury laws in terms Bentham would hardly have disowned. Ten years later an anonymous writer in a tract entitled *Considerations on the East India Trade* (1701) has no illusions about the evil of monopoly. He sees with striking clarity that the real problem is not at any cost to maintain the industries a nation actually possesses, but to have the national capital applied in the most efficient channels. So, too, Hume dismissed the Mercantile theory with the contemptuous remark that it was trying to keep water beyond its proper level. Tucker, as has been pointed out, was a free trader, and his opinion of the American war was that it was as mad as those who fought "under the peaceful Cross to recover the Holy Land"; and he urged, indeed, prophesied, the union with Ireland in the interest of commercial amity. Nor must the emphasis of the Physiocrats upon free trade be forgotten. There is no evidence now that Adam Smith owed this perception to his acquaintance with Quesnay and Turgot; but they may well have confirmed

him in it, and they show that the older
philosophy was attacked on every side.

Nor must we miss the general atmosphere of the time. On the whole his age
was a conservative one, convinced, without due reason, that happiness was independent of birth or wealth and that
natural law somehow could be made to
justify existing institutions. The poets,
like Pope, were singing of the small part
of life which kings and laws may hope to
cure; and that attitude is written in the
general absence of economic legislation
during the period. Religiously, the
Church exalted the *status quo;* and where,
as with Wesley, there was revolt, its impetus directed the mind to the source of
salvation in the individual act. It may,
indeed, be generally argued that the religious teachers acted as a social soporific.
Where riches accumulated, they could be
regarded as the blessing of God; where
they were absent their unimportance for
eternal happiness could be emphasized.
Burke's early attack on a system which
condemned "two hundred thousand inno-
cent persons . . . to so intolerable
slavery" was, in truth, a justification of

the existing order. The social question which, in the previous century, men like Bellers and Winstanley had brought into view, dropped out of notice until the last quarter of the century. There was, that is to say, no organized resistance possible to the power of individualism; and resistance was unlikely to make itself heard once the resources of the Industrial Revolution were brought into play. Men discovered with something akin to ecstasy the possibilities of the new inventions; and when the protest came against the misery they effected, it was answered that they represented the working of that natural law by which the energies of men may raise them to success. And discontent could easily, as with the saintly Wilberforce, be countered by the assertion that it was revolt against the will of God.

II

Few lives represent more splendidly than that of Adam Smith the speculative ideal of a dispassionate study of philosophy. He was fortunate in his teachers and his friends. At Glasgow he was the

pupil of Francis Hutcheson; and even if
he was taught nothing at Oxford, at least
six years of leisure gave him ample opportunity to learn. His professorship at
Glasgow not only brought him into contact with men like Hume, but also admitted him to intercourse with a group of
business men whose liberal sentiments on
commerce undoubtedly strengthened, if
they did not originate, his own liberal
views. At Glasgow, too, in 1759, he published his *Theory of Moral Sentiments,*
written with sufficient power of style to
obscure its inner poverty of thought. The
book brought him immediately a distinguished reputation from a public which
exalted elegance of diction beyond all literary virtues. The volatile Charles
Townshend made him tutor to the Duke
of Buccleuch, through whom Smith not
only secured comparative affluence for the
rest of his days, but also a French tour in
which he met at its best the most brilliant
society in Europe. The germ of his
Wealth of Nations already lay hidden in
those Glasgow lectures which Mr. Cannan has so happily recovered for us; and
it was in a moment of leisure in France

that he set to work to put them together in systematic fashion. Not, indeed, that the Frenchmen whom he met, Turgot, Quesnay and Dupont de Nemours, can be said to have done more than confirm the truths he had already been teaching. When he returned to Scotland and a competence ten years of constant labor were necessary before the *Wealth of Nations* was complete. After its publication, in 1776, Adam Smith did little save attend to the administrative duties of a minor, but lucrative office in the Customs. Until the end, indeed, he never quite gave up the hope, foreshadowed first in the *Moral Sentiments* of completing a gigantic survey of civilized institutions. But he was a slow worker, and his health was never robust. It was enough that he should have written his book and cherished friendships such as it is given to few men to possess. Hume and Burke, Millar the jurist, James Watt, Foulis the printer, Black the chemist and Hutton of geological fame — it is an enviable circle. He had known Turgot on intimate terms and visited Voltaire on Lake Geneva. Hume had told him that his book had "depth and solidity and acuteness"; the younger Pitt had consulted him on public affairs. Few men have moved amid such happy peace within the very centre of what was most illustrious in their age.

We are less concerned here with the specific economic details of the *Wealth of Nations* than with its general attitude to the State. But here a limitation upon criticism must be noted. The man of whom Smith writes is man in search of wealth; by definition the economic motive dominates his actions. Such abuse, therefore, as Ruskin poured upon him is really beside the point when his objective is borne in mind. What virtually he does is to assume the existence of a natural economic order which tends, when unrestrained by counter-tendencies, to secure the happiness of men. "That order of things which necessity imposes in general," he writes, ". . . is, in every particular country promoted by the natural inclinations of man"; and he goes on to explain what would have resulted "if human institutions had never thwarted those natural inclinations." "All systems either of preference or of restraint, there-

fore, being thus completely taken away,"
he writes again, "the obvious and simple
system of natural liberty establishes itself
of its own accord. Every man, as long as
he does not violate the laws of justice, is
left perfectly free to pursue his own interest in his own way. . . . The sovereign is completely discharged from a duty
in the attempting to perform which he
must always be exposed to innumerable
delusions, and for the proper performance
of which no human wisdom or knowledge
would ever be sufficient; the duty of su-
perintending the industry of private
people and of directing it towards the em-
ployments most suitable to the interests of
the society."

The State, in this conception has but
three functions — defence, justice and
"the duty of erecting and maintaining
certain public works and certain public institutions which it can never be for the
interest of any inidvidual, or small
number of individuals, to erect and maintain." The State, in fact, is simply to provide the atmosphere in which production
is possible. Nor does Smith conceal his
thought that the main function of justice

is the protection of property. "The affluence of the rich," he wrote, "excites the indignation of the poor, who are often both driven by want and prompted by envy to invade their possessions. It is only under the shelter of the civil magistrate that the owner of that valuable property, acquired by the labor of many years, or perhaps many successive generations, can sleep a single night in security." The attitude, indeed, is intensified by his constant sense that the capital which makes possible new productivity is the outcome of men's sacrifice; to protect it is thus to safeguard the sources of wealth itself. And even if the State is entrusted with education and the prevention of disease, this is rather for the general benefit they confer and the doubt that private enterprise would find them profitable than as the expression of a general rule. Collective effort of every kind awakened in him a deep distrust. Trade regulations such as the limitation of apprenticeship he condemned as "manifest encroachment upon the just liberty of the workman and of those who may be disposed to employ him." Even educational establishments

296 ENGLISH POLITICAL THOUGHT

are suspect on the ground — not unnatural after his own experience of Oxford
— that their possibilities of comfort may
enervate the natural energies of men.

The key to this attitude is clear enough.
The improvement of society is due, he
thinks not to the calculations of government but to the natural instincts of economic man. We cannot avoid the impulse
to better our condition; and the less its
effort is restrained the more certain it is
that happiness will result. We gain, in
fact, some sense of its inherent power
when we bear in mind the magnitude of
its accomplishment despite the folly and
extravagance of princes. Therein we
have some index of what it would achieve
if left unhindered to work out its own
destinies. Human institutions continually thwart its power; for those who build
those institutions are moved rather "by
the momentary fluctuations of affairs"
than their true nature. "That insidious
and crafty animal, vulgarly called a poli-
tician or statesman" meets little mercy for
his effort compared to the magic power of
the natural order. "In all countries where
there is a tolerable security," he writes,

"every man of common understanding will endeavor to employ whatever stock he can command in procuring either present enjoyment or future profit." Individual spontaneity is thus the root of economic good; and the real justification of the state is the protection it affords to this impulse. Man, in fact, is by nature a trader and he is bound by nature to discover the means most apt to progress.

Nor was he greatly troubled by differences of fortune. Like most of the Scottish school, especially Hutcheson and Hume, he thought that men are much alike in happiness, whatever their station or endowments. For there is a "never-failing certainty" that "all men sooner or later accommodate themselves to whatever becomes their permanent situation"; though he admits that there is a certain level below which poverty and misery go hand in hand. But, for the most part, happiness is simply a state of mind; and he seems to have had but little suspicion that differences of wealth might issue in dangerous social consequence. Men, moreover, he regarded as largely equal in their original powers; and differences of character he ascribes to the various occupations implied in the division of labor. Each man, therefore, as he follows his self-interest promotes the general happiness of society. That principle is inherent in the social order. "Every man," he wrote in the *Moral Sentiments,* "is by nature first and principally recommended to his own care" and therein he is "led by an invisible hand to promote an end which was no part of his intention." The State, that is to say, is the sum of individual goods; whereby to better ourselves is clearly to its benefit. And that desire "which comes with us from the womb and never leaves us till we go to the grave" is the more efficacious the less it is restrained by governmental artifice. For we know so well what makes us happy that none can hope to help us so much as we help ourselves.

Enlightened selfishness is thus the root of prosperity; but we must not fall into the easy fallacy which makes Smith deaf to the plaint of the poor. He urged the employer to have regard to the health and welfare of the worker, a regard which was the voice of reason and humanity. Where there was conflict between love of the *status quo* and a social good which Revolution alone could achieve, he did not, at least in the *Moral Sentiments,* hesitate to choose the latter. Order was, for the most part, indispensable; but "the greatest and noblest of all characters" he made the reformer of the State. Yet he is too impressed by the working of natural economic laws to belittle their influence. Employers, in his picture, are little capable of benevolence or charity. Their rule is the law of supply and demand and not the Sermon on the Mount. They combine without hesitation to depress wages to the lowest point of subsistence. They seize every occasion of commercial misfortune to make better terms for themselves; and the greater the poverty the more submissive do servants become so that scarcity is naturally regarded as more favorable to industry.

Obviously enough, the inner hinge of all this argument is Smith's conception of nature. Nor can there be much doubt of what he thought its inner substance. Facile distinctions such as the effort of Buckle to show that while in the *Moral*

Sentiments Adam Smith was dealing with the unselfish side of man's nature, in the *Wealth of Nations* he was dealing with a group of facts which required the abstraction of such altruistic elements, are really beside the point. Nature for Smith is simply the spontaneous action of human character unchecked by hindrances of State. It is, as Bonar has aptly said, "a vindication of the unconscious law present in the separate actions of men when these actions are directed by a certain strong personal motive." Adam Smith's argument is an assumption that the facts can be made to show the relative powerlessness of institutions in the face of economic laws grounded in human psychology. The psychology itself is relatively simple, and, at least in the *Wealth of Nations* not greatly different from the avowed assumptions of utilitarianism. He emphasizes the strength of reason in the economic field, and his sense that it enables men to judge much better of their best interests than an external authority can hope to do. And therefore the practices accomplished by this reason are those in which the impulses of men are to be found.

The order they represent is the natural order; and whatever hinders its full operation is an unwise check upon the things for which men strive.

Obviously enough, this attitude runs the grave risk of seeming to abstract a single motive — the desire for wealth — from the confused welter of human impulses and to make it dominant at the expense of human nature itself. A hasty reading of Adam Smith would, indeed, confirm that impression; and that is perhaps why he seemed to Ruskin to blaspheme human nature. But a more careful survey, particularly when the *Moral Sentiments* is borne in mind suggests a different conclusion. His attitude is implicit in the general medium in which he worked. What he was trying to do was less to emphasize that men care above all things for the pursuit of wealth than that no institutional modifications are able to destroy the power of that motive to labor. There is too much history in the *Wealth of Nations* to make tenable the hypothesis of complete abstraction. And there is even clear a sense of a nature behind his custom when he speaks of a "sacred re-

gard" for life, and urges that every man
has property in his own labor. The truth
here surely is that Smith was living in a
time of commercial expansion. What was
evident to him was the potential wealth to
be made available if the obsolete system of
restraint could be destroyed. Liberty to
him meant absence of restraint not because
its more positive aspect was concealed
from him but rather because the kind of
freedom wanted in the environment in
which he moved was exactly that for
which he made his plea. There is a hint
that freedom as a positive thing was
known to him from the fact that he relied
upon education to relieve the evils of the
division of labor. But the general context of his book required less emphasis
upon the virtues of state-interference than
upon its defects. His cue was to show
that all the benefits of regulation had been
achieved despite its interference; from
which, of course, it followed that restraint
was a matter of supererogation.

III

It would be tedious to praise the
Wealth of Nations. It may be doubtful

whether Buckle's ecstatic judgment that
it has had more influence than any other
book in the world was justified even when
he wrote; but certainly it is one of the
seminal books of the modern time. What
is more important is to note the perspective in which its main teaching was set.
He wrote in the midst of the first significant beginnings of the Industrial Revolution; and his emphatic approval of
Watt's experiments suggests that he was
not unalive to its importance. Yet it cannot in any full sense be said that the Industrial Revolution has a large part in his
book. The picture of industrial organization and its possibilities is too simple to
suggest that he had caught any far reach-
ing glimpse into the future. Industry,
for him, is still in the last stage of handi-
craft; it is a matter of skillful workmanship and not of mechanical appliance.
Capital is still the laborious result of parsimony. Credit is spoken of rather in the
tones of one who sees it less as a new instrument of finance than a dangerous attempt by the aspiring needy to scale the
heights of wealth. Profits are always a
justified return for productive labor; in-

terest the payment for the use of the
owner's past parsimony. Business is still
the middleman distributing to the consumer on a small scale. He did not, or
could not, conceive of an industry either
so vast or so depersonalized as at present.
He was rather writing of a system which,
like the politics of the eighteenth century,
had reached an equilibrium of passable
comfort. His natural order was, at
bottom, the beatification of that to which
this equilibrium tended. Its benefits
might be improved by free trade and free
workmanship; but, upon the whole, he saw
no reason to call in question its fundamental dogmas.

Therein, of course, may be found the
main secret of his omissions. The problem of labor finds no place in his book.
The things that the poor have absent from
their lives, that concept of a national min-
imum below which no State can hope to
fulfil even the meanest of its aims, of these
he has no conception. Rather the note of
the book is a quiet optimism, impressed by
the possibilities of constant improvement
which lie imbedded in the human impulse
to better itself. What he did not see is

the way in which the logical outcome of the system he describes may well be the attainment of great wealth at a price in human cost that is beyond its worth. Therein, it is clear, all individualistic theories of the state miss the true essence of the social bond. Those who came after Adam Smith saw only half his problem. He wrote a consumer's theory of value. But whereas he had in mind a happy and contented people, the economics of Ricardo and Malthus seized upon a single element in human nature as that which alone the State must serve. Freedom from restraint came ultimately to mean a judgment upon national well-being in terms of the volume of trade. "It is not with happiness," said Nassau Senior, "but with wealth that I am concerned as a political economist; and I am not only justified in omitting, but am perhaps bound to omit, all considerations which have no influence upon wealth."

In such an aspect, it was natural for the balance of investigation to swing towards the study of the technique of production; and with the growing importance of capital, as machinery was introduced, the

worker, without difficulty, became an adjunct, easily replaced, to the machine.
What was remembered then was the side of Adam Smith which looked upon enlightened selfishness as the key to social good. Regulation became anathema even when the evils it attempted to restrain were those which made the mass of the people incapable of citizenship. Even national education was regarded as likely to destroy initiative; or, as a pauper's dole which men of self-respect would regard with due abhorrence. The State, in short, ceased to concern itself with justice save insofar as the administration of a judicial code spelled the protection of the new industrial system. Nothing is more striking in the half-century after Adam Smith than the optimism of the economist and the business man in contrast to the hopeless despair of labor. That men can organize to improve their lot was denied with emphasis, so that until Francis Place even the workers themselves were half-convinced. The manufacturers were the State; and the whole intellectual strength of economics was massed to prove the rightness of the equation. The literature

of protest, men like Hall and Thompson, Hodgskin and Bray, exerted no influence upon the legislation of the time; and Robert Owen was deemed an amiable eccentric rather than the prophet of a new hope. The men who succeeded, as Wilberforce, carried out to the letter the unstated assumptions of Puritan economics. The poor were consigned to a God whose dictates were by definition beneficent; and if they failed to understand the curious incidence of his rewards that was because his ways were inscrutable. No one who reads the tracts of writers like Harriet Martineau can fail to see how pitiless was the operation of this attitude. Life is made a struggle beneficent, indeed, but deriving its ultimate meaning from the misery incident to it. The tragedy is excused because the export-trade increases in its volume. The iron law of wages, the assumed transition of every energetic worker to the ranks of wealth, the danger lest the natural ability of the worker to better his condition be sapped by giving to him that which his self-respect can better win — these became the unconscious assumptions of all economic discussion.

In all this, as in the foundation with
which Adam Smith provided it, we must
not miss the element of truth that it contains. No poison is more subtly destructive of the democratic State than
paternalism; and the release of the creative impulses of men must always be the
coping-stone of public policy. Adam
Smith is the supreme representative of a
tradition which saw that release effected
by individual effort. Where each man
cautiously pursued the good as he saw it,
the realization was bound, in his view, to
be splendid. A population each element
of which was active and alert to its economic problems could not escape the
achievement of greatness. All that is
true; but it evades the obvious conditions
we have inherited. For even when the
psychological inadequacies of Smith's attitude are put aside, we can judge his
theory in the light of the experience it
summarizes. Once it is admitted that the
object of the State is the achievement of
the good life, the final canon of politics is
bound to be a moral one. We have to inquire into the dominant conception of the
good life, the number of those upon whom
it is intended that good shall be conferred.

In the light of this conception it is obvious enough that Smith's view is impossible. No mere conflict of private interests, however pure in motive, seems able to achieve a harmony of interest between the members of the State. Liberty, in the sense of a positive and equal opportunity for self-realization, is impossible save upon the basis of the acceptance of certain minimal standards which can get accepted only through collective effort. Smith did not see that in the processes of politics what gets accepted is not the will that is at every moment a part of the state-purpose, but the will of those who in fact operate the machinery of government. In the half-century after he wrote the men who dominated political life were, with the best intentions, moved by motives at most points unrelated to the national well-being. The fellow-servant doctrine would never have obtained acceptance in a state where, as he thought, employer and workman stood upon an equal footing. Opposition to the Factory Acts would never have developed in a community where it was realized that below certain standards of subsistence the very concept of humanity is impossible. Modern achievement implies a training in the tools of life; and that, for most, is denied even in our own day to the vast majority of men. In the absence of legislation, it is certain that those who employ the services of men will be their political masters; and it will follow that their Acts of Parliament will be adapted to the needs of property. That shrinkage of the purpose of the State will mean for most not merely hardship but degradation of all that makes life worthy. Upon those stunted existences, indeed, a wealthy civilization may easily be builded. Yet it will be a civilization of slaves rather than of men.

The individualism, that is to say, for which Adam Smith was zealous demands a different institutional expression from that which he gave it. We must not assume an *a priori* justification for the forces of the past. The customs of men may represent the thwarting of the impulses of the many at the expense of the few not less easily than they may embody a general desire; and it is surely a mistaken usage to dignify as natural whatever may happen to have occurred. A man may find self-realization not less in working for the common good than in the limited satisfaction of his narrow desire for material advancement. And that, indeed, is the starting-point of modern effort. Our liberty means the consistent expression of our personality in media where we find people like-minded with ourselves in their conception of social life. The very scale of civilization implies collective plans and common effort. The constant revision of our basic notions was inevitable immediately science was applied to industry. There was thus no reason to believe that the system of individual interests for which Smith stood sponsor was more likely to fit requirements of a new time than one which implied the national regulation of business enterprise. The danger in every period of history is lest we take our own age as the term in institutional evolution. Private enterprise has the sanction of prescription; but since the Industrial Revolution the chief lesson we have had to learn is the unsatisfactory character of that title. History is an unenviable record of bad metaphysics used

to defend obsolete systems. It took almost a century after the publication of
the *Wealth of Nations* for men to realize
that its axioms represented the experience
of a definite time. Smith thought of freedom in the terms most suitable to his generation and stated them with a largeness
of view which remains impressive even at
a century's distance.

But nothing is more certain in the history of political philosophy than that the
problem of freedom changes with each
age. The nineteenth century sought release from political privilege; and it built
its success upon the system prepared by
its predecessor. It can never be too
greatly emphasized that in each age the
substance of liberty will be found in what
the dominating forces of that age most
greatly want. With Locke, with Smith,
with Hegel and with Marx, the ultimate
hypothesis is always the summary of some
special experience universalized. That
does not mean that the past is worthless.
Politics, as Seeley said, are vulgar unless
they are liberalized by history; and a state
which failed to see itself as a mosaic of
ancestral institutions would build its

novelties upon foundations of sand. Suspicions of collective effort in the eighteenth century ought not to mean
suspicion in the twentieth; to think in such
fashion is to fall into the error for which
Lassalle so finely criticized Hegel. It is
as though one were to confound the accidental phases of the history of property
with the philosophic basis of property itself. From such an error it is the task of
history above all to free us. For it records
the ideals and doubts of earlier ages as a
perennial challenge to the coming time.

The rightness of this attitude admits of
proof in terms of the double tradition to
which Adam Smith gave birth. On the
one hand he is the founder of the classic
political economy. With Ricardo, the
elder Mill and Nassau Senior, the main
preoccupation is the production of wealth
without regard to its moral environment;
and the state for them is merely an en-
gine to protect the atmosphere in which
business men achieve their labors. There
is nothing in them of that fine despair
which made Stuart Mill welcome socialism
itself rather than allow the continuance of
the new capitalist system. Herein the

State is purged of moral purpose; and the utilitarian method achieves the greatest happiness by insisting that the technique of production must dominate all other circumstances. Until the Reform Act of 1867, the orthodox economists remained unchallenged. The use of the franchise was only beginning to be understood. The "new model" of trade unionism had not yet been tested in the political field. But it was discovered impossible to act any longer upon the assumptions of the abstract economic man. The infallible sense of his own interest was discovered to be without basis in the facts for the simple reason that the instruments of his perception obviously required training if they were to be applied to a complex world. Individualism, in the old, utilitarian sense, passed away because it failed to build a State wherein a channel of expression might be found for the creative energies of humble men.

It is only within the last two decades that we have begun to understand the inner significance of the protest against this economic liberalism. Adam Smith had declared the source of value to lie in

labor; and, at the moment of its deepest
agony, there were men willing to point
the moral of his tale. That it represented
an incautious analysis was, for them, unimportant beside the fact that it opened
once more a path whereby economics
could be reclaimed for moral science. For
if labor was the source of value, as Bray
and Thompson pointed out, it seemed as
though degradation was the sole payment
for its services. They did not ask whether
the organization they envisaged was eco-
nomically profitable, but whether it was
ethically right. No one can read the history of these years and fail to understand
their uncompromising denial of its rightness. Their negation fell upon unheeding
ears; but twenty years later, the tradition
for which they stood came into Marx's
hands and was fashioned by him into an
interpretation of history. With all its
faults of statement and of emphasis, the
doctrine of the English socialists has been,
in later hands, the most fruitful hypothesis of modern politics. It was a deliberate effort, upon the basis of Adam
Smith's ideas, to create a commonwealth
in the interests of the masses. Wealth, in

its view, was less the mere production of
goods than the accumulated happiness of
humble men. The impulses it praised and
sought through state-action to express
were, indeed, different from those upon
which Smith laid emphasis; and he would
doubtless have stood aghast at the way in
which his thought was turned to ends of
which he did not dream. Yet he can
hardly have desired a greater glory. He
thus made possible not only knowledge of
a State untrammelled in its economic life
by moral considerations; but also the road
to those categories wherein the old conception of co-operative effort might find
a new expression. Those who trod in his
footsteps may have repudiated the ideal
for which he stood, but they made possible
a larger hope in which he would have been
proud and glad to share.

BIBLIOGRAPHY

This bibliography makes no pretence to completeness. It attempts only to enumerate the more obvious sources that an interested reader would care to examine.

GENERAL

LESLIE STEPHEN. *History of English Thought in the Eighteenth Century*. 1876. Vol. II, Chapters IX and X.

W. E. H. LECKY. *History of England in the Eighteenth Century.*

A. L. SMITH. *Political Philosophy in England in the Seventeenth and Eighteenth Centuries* in the *Cambridge Modern History*. Vol. VI, Chapter XXIII.

J. BONAR. *Philosophy and Political Economy*. Chapters V–IX.

F. W. MAITLAND. *An Historical Sketch of Liberty and Equality* in *Collected Papers*. Vol. I.

CHAPTER II

JOHN LOCKE. *Works* (Eleventh Edition), 10 volumes. London, 1812.

H. R. FOX-BOURNE. *Life of John Locke*. London, 1876.

T. H. GREEN. *The Principles of Political Obligation* in *Collected Works*. Vol. II. London, 1908.

PETER, LORD KING. *The Life and Letters of John Locke.* London, 1858.

SIR F. POLLOCK. *Locke's Theory of the State* in *Proc. Brit. Acad.* Vol. I. London, 1904.

S. P. LAMPRECHT. *The Moral and Political Philosophy of Locke*. New York, 1918.

A. A. SEATON. *The Theory of Toleration under the Later Stuarts*. Cambridge, 1911.

J. N. FIGGIS. *The Divine Right of Kings*. Cambridge, 1914.

317

CHAPTER III

JEREMY COLLIER. *The History of Passive Obedience.* London, 1689.

WILLIAM SHERLOCK. *The Case of Resistance.* London, 1684.

CHARLES LESLIE. *The Case of the Regale* (Collected Works). Vol. III, p. 291.
    The Rehearsal.
    The New Association.
    Cassandra.
    The Finishing Stroke.
    Obedience to Civil Government Clearly Stated.
    The Best Answer.
    The Best of All.

SAMUEL GRASCOM. *A Brief Answer.*

E. SHELLINGFLEET. *A Vindication of their Majesties Authoritie.*

B. SHOWER. *A Letter to a Convocation Man.*

W. WAKE. *The Authority of Christian Princes.*
    The State of the Church (1703).

FRANCIS ATTERBURY. *Rights, Powers and Privileges of an English Convocation* (1701).

BENJAMIN HOADLY. *Origins of Civil Government* (1710).
    Preservative Against Nonjurors (1716).
    Works, 3 vols. London (1773).

WILLIAM LAW. *A Defence of Church Principles* (ed. Gore). Edinburgh, 1904.

W. WARBURTON. *Alliance between Church and State* (1736).

J. H. OVERTON. *The Nonjurors.* New York, 1903.

T. LATHBURY. *History of Convocation.* London, 1842.

CHAPTER IV

BERKELEY. *Essay Towards Preventing the Ruin of Great Britain* (1721).

H. ST. JOHN (Viscount Bolingbroke). *Works.* 5 vols. London, 1754.

LORD EGMONT. *Faction detected by the Evidence of Facts* (1742).

DAVID HUME. *Inquiry Concerning the Principles of Morals* (1752).

Essays. (1742–1752) ed. Green & Grose. London, 1876.

W. SICHEL. *Life of Bolingbroke.* 2 vols. 1900–4.

J. CHURTON COLLINS. *Bolingbroke and Voltaire in England.*

J. HILL BURTON. *Life of Hume.*

CHAPTER V

MONTESQUIEU. *L'Esprit des Lois* (1748).

J. J. ROUSSEAU. *Du Contrat Social* (1762). See ed. by Vaughan, 1918.

JOHN BROWN. *Estimate of the Manners and Principles of the Times* (1757).

ADAM FERGUSON. *Essay on the History of Civil Society* (1767).

WILLIAM BLACKSTONE. *Commentaries* (1765–9).

JEREMY BENTHAM. *A Fragment on Government* (1776). Ed. F. C. Montague, 1891.

J. DE LOLME. *The Constitution of England* (1775).

ROBERT WALLACE. *Various Prospects* (1761).

JOSEPH PRIESTLEY. *Essay on the First Principles of Government* (1768).

RICHARD PRICE. *Observations on Civil Liberty* (1776). *Additional Observations* (1777).

WILLIAM OGILVIE. *The Right of Property in Land* (1781). Ed. Macdonald, 1891.

JOSIAH TUCKER. *Treatise on Civil Government* (1781).

SAMUEL JOHNSON. *Taxation No Tyranny* (1775).

M. BEER. *History of British Socialism* (1919).

JAMES BOSWELL. *Life of Samuel Johnson* (1791).

CHAPTER VI

EDMUND BURKE. *Collected Works.* London, 1808.

JOHN MORLEY. *Edmund Burke* (1867). *Life of Burke* (1887).

J. MACCUNN. *The Political Philosophy of Burke* (1908).

JUNIUS. *Letters* (1769–72). London, 1812.

THOMAS PAINE. *The Rights of Man* (1791–2).

JAMES MACKINTOSH. *Vendiciæ Gallicæ* (1791).

CHAPTER VII

CHARLES DAVENANT. *Works.* London, 1771.

SIR DUDLEY NORTH. *A Discourse upon Trade* (1691).

ADAM SMITH. *Theory of Moral Sentiments* (1759).
Wealth of Nations (1776).
Lectures on Justice and Police. (Ed. Cannan, 1896).

W. R. SCOTT. *Life of Francis Hutcheson* (1900).

JOHN RAE. *Life of Adam Smith* (1895).

W. BAGEHOT. *Adam Smith as a Person* in *Coll. Works.* Vol. VII.

F. W. HIRST. *Adam Smith* (1904).

W. HASBACH. *Untersuchungen über Adam Smith* (1891).

J. BONAR. *A Catalogue of Adam Smith's Library* (1894).

T. CLIFFE LESLIE. *Adam Smith* in *Essays in Moral and Political Philosophy* (1879).

E. TROELTSCH. *Die Sociallehren der Christlichen Kirchen* (1912).

INDEX

Addison, 69
Andrewes, 83
Ashley, 33–4
Atterbury, 102
Austin, 62

Bagehot, 9, 249
Barbeyrac, 68
Barrow, 84
Bellarmine, 83, 121
Bentham, 23, 62, 72, 151, 157, 175, 194
Berkeley, 10, 129
Blackstone, 163–4, 174f
Bolingbroke, 69, 131f
Bonald, 277
Bonar, 300
Bonwicke, 82
Boswell, 209
Bray, 307, 315
Brown (J.), 168
Brown (R.), 52
Burke, 7, 8, 16, 30, 157, 159, 166, 221f, 286
Burnet, 80, 87, 93
Busher, 52

Cartwright, 97
Chatham, 132, 167, 188, 262
Chillingworth, 52
Chubb, 128
Coleridge, 277
Collier, 84n
Cowper, 20
Crabbe, 20

Dalrymple, 8
Darwin, 67
Davenant, 283, 287
Defoe, 8, 128, 132
Dicey, 175, 179
Disraeli, 132
Divine Right, 7, 30
Dodwell, 82
Dupont de Nemours, 292

Egmont, 142
Eldon, 159

Ferguson, 172–4
Fielding, 160
Filmer, 7, 38

Galsworthy, 171–2
George III, 13, 15, 158, 188, 213f
Godwin, 10, 163, 222, 276
Goldsmith, 19, 223
Goodman, 57
Grascom, 86
Gray, 160
Green (T. H.), 61, 279

Haldane, 126
Hales, 52
Halifax, 8, 27
Hall, 17, 307
Hamilton (J. L. & B.), 19
Harrington, 147
Hegel, 249, 277, 212–3
Hickes, 83

Hoadly, 9, 22, 69, 107f
Hubbes, 8, 16, 30, 40f, 72,
  91, 278, 284
Hodgskin, 17, 307
Holmes (O. W.), 63n, 269
Holt, 14
Hooker, 44
Hotman, 57, 68
Hume, 8, 11, 71, 92, 143f,
  278, 284, 297
Hutcheson, 11, 153, 155,
  291, 297

Independents, 40

Jackson, 84
James II, 24f, 35
Johnson (Dr.), 18, 210f,
  223, 230
Junius, 21, 219

Keble, 82
Kerr, 82
Knox, 57, 83, 97

Lassalle, 313
Laud, 285
Law, 22, 108f
Leslie, 80, 85, 88, 90, 97,
  104, 132
Locke, 7, 11, 21, 29–76, 79,
  197, 207, 273, 287
de Lolme, 10, 183f

Mackintosh, 269
Madison, 63
Maine, 66, 249
Maistre, 91, 252, 273
Malthus, 305
Mandeville, 129, 284
Mariana, 57
Martin, 69
Marx, 312, 315
Melville, 121
Mill, 157

Milton, 52
Molyneux, 68
Montesquieu, 12, 63, 160f,
  173, 183
Morley, 132, 223

Newton, 37
Newman, 81, 122, 125
North, 287

Ogilvie, 199f
Owen, 17, 307
Oxford Movement, 81

Paine, 202, 269
Paley, 157
Pattison, 10
Penn, 58
Place, 306
Pope, 69, 128, 132
Price, 196f
Priestley, 72, 190f
Proast, 64
Prynne, 8, 55
Pufendorf, 68
Pulteney, 217

Quesnay, 288, 292

Renan, 249
Ricardo, 305
Richardson, 160
Richardson (S.), 52
Rousseau, 8, 74, 162f, 188,
  197, 276
Royer-Collard, 226
Ruskin, 293, 301

Sanderson, 84
Savigny, 249, 277
Seeley, 312
Selden, 9
Senior, 304
Separation of Powers, 63f
Shaftesbury, 11, 128, 155

Sherlock (T.), 108
Sherlock (W.), 87
Shower, 99
Sidney, 7, 57
Smith (Adam), 9, 16, 152, 195, 258, 281f
Smith (A. L.), 140
Snape, 108
Social Contract, 57
Spelman, 9
Spence, 202
Stammler, 60
Steele, 284
Stephen (F.), 65
Stephen (L.), 108, 223
Stillingfleet, 37, 87, 93
Suarez, 57

Taylor, 52, 57
Temple, 283

Thompson, 307, 215
Tindal, 123
Tocqueville, 254
Toleration, 52, 64
Tucker, 71, 206f, 288
Turgot, 288, 292

Voltaire, 12, 132, 160

Wake, 80, 100f
Wallace, 188
Walpole, 13, 21, 128–30
Warburton, 69, 118f, 192
Wilberforce, 290
Wilkes, 167, 188, 220
William III, 25f
Williams (Roger), 52
Woolston, 128
Wordsworth, 277